Hive Management History Series: No. 73

DONALDSON BROWN

Some Reminiscences of an Industrialist

by

DONALDSON BROWN

Introduction by Ernest Dale

EASTON
HIVE PUBLISHING COMPANY
1977

Copyright © 1977 by Hive Publishing Company

Library of Congress Cataloging in Publication Data

Brown, Donaldson, 1885-1965.
   Some reminiscences of an industrialist.
   (Management history series ; no. 73)
   Reprint of the 1958 ed.
   1. Brown, Donaldson, 1885-1965. 2. Businessmen—
United States—Correspondence, reminiscences, etc.
I. Title.
HC102.5.B7A36   1975   338'.092'4 [B]   74-34383
ISBN 0-87960-109-4

Manufactured in the United States of America

TO

Greta, my wife

*steadfast companion and wonderful mother,
whose good sense, affection and loyalty
helped to make the bad times easier —
and the good times meaningful.*

CONTENTS

	Page
Introduction	i
Foreword	1
Chapter 1. Background – Boyhood and College	7
Chapter 2. Beginnings of a Business Career	17
Chapter 3. R = T x P	26
Chapter 4. New Challenges at General Motors	45
Chapter 5. Basic Policies of Corporate Management	59
Chapter 6. Banks, Labor and Government	72
Chapter 7. War, Post-War and Retirement	103
Chapter 8. Looking Ahead	109

APPENDIX

1. "A Letter From A Father To His Sons"	121
2. GM Monthly Report Form	129
3. "Pricing Policy in Relation to Financial Control"	130
4. "A Statement of General Motors Corporation's Basic Policies Governing Its Relations With Factory Employees"	158
5. Decentralized Operations and Responsibilities With Coordinated Control	167

Introduction

The charting technique that the Du Pont Company utilizes for financial control of its operations constitutes one of the best measures of management effectiveness ever devised. In a single year, the company may be called upon to make a hundred or more presentations on the subject to outside groups, which include both associations and individuals.

Although this technique is still new to many managements, it was actually devised well over a half-century ago by the man who is the subject of this volume, Donaldson Brown, and it is still essentially the same as when he devised it. In brief, it is based on the formula (or "mathematical model" as it would be called today):

$$R = T \times P$$

Here R represents the rate of return on capital, which—as Brown stated—"is a final and fundamental measure of industrial efficiency." T stands for the rate of turnover of invested capital, and P for the percentage of profit on sales. Both T and P, of course, are made up of more than one component, as Brown showed in his original explanation of the formula (which is included in this book).

In his autobiography, the late Alfred P. Sloan, Jr., chief executive of General Motors for more than 30 years, wrote of Brown's plan, which was introduced at GM when Brown joined the company:

"The early return-on-investment form, which with some modifications is still used in General Motors, was the first step in educating our operating personnel in the meaning and importance of rate of return as a standard of performance. It provided executives with a quantitative basis for sound decision-making and thereby laid the foundation for what was to be one of General Motors' most important characteristics, namely, its effort to achieve open-minded communication and objective consideration of facts."[1]

---

1. *My Years With General Motors* (edited by John McDonald with Catherine Stevens) Doubleday & Company, Inc., Garden City, N.Y., 1964, p. 143.

The R = T x P formula might be termed a major breakthrough in the field of systematic management, but it was only one of many important contributions Brown made at Du Pont and later at General Motors, where he served as vice president in charge of finance and as vice chairman of the board of directors. Other contributions included:

1. A pricing policy based on a standard volume designed to produce an acceptable rate of return on investment averaged over a period that included both good and bad years, provided the company's products were at least equal to those of competitors in styling and quality. The "standard volume" concept was based on the idea that the company could not expect a return on excess capacity.

In his analysis, Brown made use of the theory of marginal costs—and may have been the first industry man to point out that it could be utilized as a basis for practical decision-making. ("If volume is susceptible of increase by price reduction, then a price reduction is desirable, provided the added volume affords an increase in aggregate profit in excess of the economic cost of the additional capital requirement.") At any rate, one long-term GM executive states: "It seems to me that GM people were talking intelligently along these lines at a time when it (marginal theory) was an economic abstraction for most industrialists."

2. Pioneering work in the use of economic forecasts. When Brown joined the treasurer's department at Du Pont, he engaged a consulting economist to provide advice on trends in the economy that might be expected to affect the company's business. Later, at General Motors, the same economist and several analysts were employed.

3. Identification of "hidden inventory"—that is, inventory in the hands of dealers. As Brown reports in the reminiscences that follow, he had a number of discussions with Herbert Hoover, then Secretary of Commerce, on this subject; and they both agreed that the automobile industry was in a better position to control hidden inventory than many other industries were. In automobiles, only the dealers stood between the manufacturer and the ultimate consumer, whereas in steel, for example, there were many inter-

mediaries—fabricators of various types and merchandise suppliers.

Matters came to a head in 1924 when Brown stated that the studies of car registrations made by one of his staff groups, known as the "central office sales section," showed that there was overproduction, and the general sales manager of one of the divisions insisted there was not, that he knew more about the stocks in the field than those in the central office possibly could.

Brown's view was vindicated when he and Sloan went on a field trip to visit dealers and found excessive inventories of cars. From this, after group discussions, there emerged a plan to get reports from dealers every ten days, a practice that was later adopted by the entire industry.

4. The development of plans that would insure a uniform system of accounting for dealers.

Although probably not the originator of the idea, Brown also placed his influence strongly on the side of the General Motors concept of "decentralized operations and coordinated control," and was one of those who helped to make it a reality as well as a slogan. Some of his contributions to coordinated control have been mentioned, but he was equally insistent on decentralized operations with decision making powers delegated as far down in the hierarchy as possible. His viewpoint on this is well expressed in his comments on the plan for the ten-day dealer reports:

"It will be observed that the sales and distribution group did not 'order' adoption of the intended procedure; it possessed no administrative power to do so. What it did was to present available facts, and bring to the attention of the operating divisions the procedures and principles which seemed best capable of improving dealer relations and the general economics of distribution and sales. Its function might be described as 'factual persuasion.'"

For Brown "factual persuasion" was almost a fetish. He once wrote to one of his fellow directors:

"In the course of time, there came to be endless discussions and arguments over how the governing committees should be organized. ----(one of the men who served as president of the corporation after Sloan became chairman of the board) always contended he did not care how big might be any committee of which he could serve as chairman. 'If chairman,' he would say, 'I can sell the committee, regardless of its size, on the right thing to do.' I used to shudder over the reflection of this dangerous concept in the face of our long continuous struggles to get at the facts bearing upon policy formulation through the laborious processes of free expressions of knowledge and opinions around the council table."

Again, in a letter to Sloan in 1953, in which he discussed a presentation Sloan had made to the financial committee regarding the prospective retirement dates for high-level personnel and the need to plan for replacements, Brown wrote of his fear that future top men might whittle away the decentralization. He pointed out:

"It is not easy . . . for a high ranking executive, conscious of the responsibilities resting on him, to refrain from dictating to subordinates when he himself has convictions of what should be done in a specific case. It is difficult for him to rest content in accepting delayed action. Experience over the years in General Motors, however, has demonstrated beyond question the value of delayed action until convictions have come to be formed in the minds of the administrative management directly concerned. Policy group meetings as well as meetings of the Administration Committee (or Operations Committee) have been conducted largely on the plan of forum discussions where the main purpose has been to assure the wholehearted acceptance of a formulated procedure on the part of the immediate management as being in the best interests of the business."

Brown's pricing plan has been criticized as "administered pricing" but it was not administered in the sense that it called for any collusion with competitors or any imitation of them. Every business man prices his products to yield a profit over and above costs—otherwise, he cannot stay in business very long. Brown's plan called for administration of prices only in the sense that good administration should be applied to pricing as to everything else—it mitigated the instability caused by the underabsorption of overhead in times of low volume and overabsorption in times of high volume.

In fact, the formula often operated to keep prices down rather than to raise them. Before the "standard volume" concept was introduced, managers frequently raised prices when volume fell off because they felt that wider unit margins were "needed" to make the profit they believed they should make.

Later, in the period following World War II, when there was a black market in cars because the industry could not immediately meet the rising demand, Brown agreed only reluctantly that the divisions should be permitted (but not ordered) to raise prices above the standard formula — he was very distressed by the fact that some in the industry were leaning in the direction of charging all the traffic would bear. And the arguments that induced him to agree to a temporary abandonment of the formula were persuasive:

(a) If important competitors raised their prices, they would later be forced to reduce them when supply caught up with demand, and GM might appear at a disadvantage if it did not institute price cuts also — even though it had not enjoyed the same abnormal profits during the shortages.

(b) If GM prices were very far below those of competitors, it might appear to the general public that its products were less valuable. (And it is true that many customers judge quality by price. Sometimes a product that will not sell at a low price wins consumer acceptance after the price is raised.)

At no time in his life was Brown in favor of "all the traffic will bear" in the matter of pricing. Once when he was a salesman for Du Pont, he succeeded in getting an order despite the fact that Du Pont's price was higher than that of a competitor. After the contract had been signed, Brown went to his boss and suggested that Du Pont fill the order at the competitor's price, even though the customer had agreed to the higher figure. His immediate boss agreed, but the general sales manager did not.

One of Brown's associates once said: "Brown projects a

perfect situation and then works backwards; whereas, I start with what exists and then come up with a tolerable solution." Brown's pricing policy was simply an example of this working backwards from what ought to be to methods of bringing it about. But his solutions were always realistic because he had a very incisive mind, particularly in financial matters. Another associate recalled that when Brown first began collecting financial data and ratios from Du Pont divisions, he received a number of reports, threw a glance at each, and then pounced on one figure and stated that it was wrong. It took the accounting department six weeks to find out why.

Associates also recall that he thought matters through so carefully that he was often able to bring to their attention facets of problems (e.g., human or political aspects) that had not occurred to them, and that although he was primarily a "thinker-upper," he was a capable decision maker.

In addition, many of them praised his character as well as his intelligence. One of them recalled, with entire agreement, a statement that W. Grimes of the *Wall Street Journal* once made about Brown: "This man never had a small thought." The associate added: "His greatness was not only in technical competence; he was also a great human guy, very considerate and relaxed.

"I remember that when I was temporarily 'on loan' to the government, there was some retrenchment at GM, and I was a little worried for fear that I might lose my place and be relegated to a less important job when I returned. I had not spoken of this to anyone, but Brown realized that I might be anxious and wrote me a letter reassuring me."

I met Don Brown in 1954, through John Lee Pratt, who was for many years second-in-command at General Motors Corporation and one of those who contributed largely to its prosperity and success. Mr. Pratt felt that it was essential for any student of Du Pont and GM to meet Don Brown because he, more than any one else, was responsible for many of the basic concepts and principles underlying the management of both companies. Charles E. Wilson, later chief executive of General Motors and then Defense secretary, during World War II used to refer to Brown as the company's "thinker-upper."

My first contact with Brown was in connection with the suit brought by the Department of Justice to force Du Pont to give up its investment in General Motors on the ground that the Du Pont men on the GM board were in a position to force GM to purchase Du Pont products. The Department did not charge that the Du Pont directors had ever used their power in this way; there was no evidence that they had. It was the mere possibility that led the Supreme Court to order the relationship between the two companies dissolved.

Certainly, Don Brown would have been strongly opposed to any attempt on the part of Du Pont to force its products on GM. Long before antitrust laws were as firmly enforced as they are today, he was opposed to many common practices that violated the spirit of the laws. For example, he was very much against reciprocity ("you buy from me and I'll buy from you") and opposed also to any collusion with competitors. In fact, he quit one job because his boss told him that he should be "less aggressive" in his selling efforts and leave more of the market to a competitor—which happened to be the parent company of the firm he worked for, although that fact was not generally known.

I agreed with Brown that the dissociation of Du Pont and GM was not in the public interest because it furthered the divorce of ownership and control, a trend that has been evident in big business for some time and which leaves management, whose interest may be contrary to that of stockholders, in complete control.

I felt that it was important that there be some check on managerial power, by either individuals or companies whose stockholdings were large enough to make their interests identical with those of other stockholders, that there should be someone to exercise what Alfred P. Sloan, Jr. once christened "veto power" over the managers, to whom salaries and bonuses might be more important than dividends or capital gains on any small amounts of stock they possessed. (Apparently, Du Pont had exercised its veto power only three times during its tenure, which lasted from 1920 to 1959, but as long as stockholder interests have the power to exercise a check, the effect is the same.)

Brown was interested in my ideas on the importance of making management accountable to owners in some way and we conducted an extensive correspondence over the next ten years. A partial result of this exchange was a book, *The Great Organizers,*[2] and a monograph, "Hamilton McFarland Barksdale and the Du Pont Contributions to Systematic Management."[3]

Brown was a very meticulous correspondent and after his retirement he typed all his letters, even very long ones, himself. His correspondence was always very precise and helpful and usually encouraging and illuminating. It was his ability to conceptualize, explain, and teach that made him so influential in the companies in which he worked. Although I met Don Brown a number of times, like others I found it easier to correspond with him than to discuss matters face-to-face, for he was shy and modest to the extreme.

Toward the end of his life, in answer to my inquiries, he admitted that he had thought about publishing his reflections and an account of his business experience. Others, including Alfred P. Sloan, Jr. had suggested the same thing to him. Eventually he did write his life story but had it privately printed only for his family and friends, and the supply was quickly exhausted. (My own copy has been constantly on loan to executives who found it fascinating reading and full of good ideas succinctly expressed.) In response to several suggestions on my part that his reminiscences be made available to a wider audience through a commercial publisher, he wrote (June 4, 1965):

"I'm quite flattered by your wanting to publish that book of mine. As I said over the 'phone, I would be glad if there is something in its content that would be of educational value,

---

2. McGraw-Hill Book Company, New York, 1960.
3. With Charles Meloy, published as an article in *The Business History Review,* Summer, 1962, pp. 127-152, and later reprinted in Ernest Dale (ed.) *Readings in Management: Landmarks and New Frontiers.* McGraw-Hill Book Company, New York, 1965, pp. 4-7.

and I am pleased to leave the matter entirely in your hands. It would be my idea that you might reconstruct the book by way of leaving out passages that have no bearing on the educational purpose, and add things which might broaden its usefulness. If you find anything in the other raft of letters and papers I sent you some time ago that might fit in by way of elaboration, that would be O.K. by me." But in his modesty, he said later: "There would be no need of actual quotations," and added that his correspondence with other directors and executives of Du Pont and GM "might strike a note in your mind worthy of some extended treatment . . . if you were thinking of writing another book dealing with management."

There were more letters and some meetings in the hope of pulling together some joint product. But death intervened too soon. Hence it was my feeling, which was shared by the executors of his estate, that Donaldson Brown's own work should stand on its own, apart from editing.

Actually, I have done only a minimum of editing on the book and on the papers presented in the form of appendices to this volume. I might, of course, have removed references, such as those of "Negro retainers," which may fall strangely on modern ears. But Brown's words do not indicate any endorsement or justification of an inferior position for the Negro; he was merely trying to recreate—for family and friends the vanished age into which he was born and the conditions surrounding his early life. His book must be read with this in mind.

Donaldson Brown was born in Baltimore in 1885 and spent much of his early life there and in West Virginia. He grew up in what was essentially the "Old South;" a region that still largely retained the ideas of an earlier period. It was an age in which, as Brown's autobiography shows, one drove to the doctor in a horse-and-buggy and found him hoeing his cornfield; an age in which it was practically taken for granted that at least one of the young people would have typhoid fever every summer.

Brown was a descendant of a Scotch-Irish family who immigrated to Virginia from New Jersey in the 1700's. His paternal grandfather was a Princeton graduate and an attorney, who died at the age of 34, but left behind a letter to his sons, from which Brown, a grandson, derived considerable inspiration.

Don studied electrical engineering at Virginia Polytechnic Institute, and later went to Cornell, but he was forced to go to work at the age of 17 because his father had failed in business. Characteristically, Brown obtained his first job as a result of a new idea: When he was about ten years old, he and his friends spent a great deal of time experimenting with telegraphs and other electrical apparatus. The manager of the Baltimore General Electric Company offered a prize to the member of the group who came up with the best new application of electricity. Brown won the prize, and later when he needed a job, the manager recommended him for a position with a GE subsidiary.

At 19, he was sales manager for two states, and it was here that he was warned to become "less aggressive," and so began looking out for another position. After an abortive attempt to start a business of his own, he joined the Du Pont Company, where he became a salesman for the contractor's division. Later, Hamilton McFarland Barksdale, the general manager the company, invited him to join the general office staff "to attend to analytical matters."

Eventually, Brown married Barksdale's daughter, Greta, which was perhaps an indication of his ability to persist in the face of difficulties. One of Brown's contemporaries who later served as a high official in Du Pont and then in General Motors, recalls that he, too, was greatly attracted by Barksdale's daughter, but gave up his pursuit when her father insisted on making a third on all dates. Such chaperonage was not common, even in the early years of the century, but Barksdale, whose ideas on business were often far ahead of his time, was rather old-fashioned in his ideas on social relations.

Brown's big opportunity came in 1914 when Coleman du Pont, then president of the company, asked for a report on the performance of the several operating departments. It was then that Brown devised his formula: $R = T \times P$, and as a result, Du Pont suggested to John J. Raskob, then treasurer of the company, that Brown belonged in the financial department.

Brown joined the financial department as assistant treasurer and from then on his rise was rapid. Four years later, when Raskob became vice president, Brown succeeded him as treasurer. Then when Du Pont was forced to bail out GM, which was in serious financial difficulties in 1920 because over-expansion found it unprepared for the recession of 1920-21, Brown transferred to the automobile company. He became GM's Vice President in Charge of Finance and a member of the board of directors and the finance committee. At GM he introduced his $R = T \times P$ method of judging divisional performance and other methods of coordination through financial controls.

General Motors already had the decentralized operations that Brown, Alfred P. Sloan, Jr., John Lee Pratt, and others of the group that took over thought it so important to preserve, but it was entirely lacking in any form of coordinated control. At a meeting of division heads, for example, one manager observed to another: "I see you raised your prices the other day; I think I'll raise mine tomorrow." John Lee Pratt recalled later that the division heads obtained appropriations by a form of logrolling— when one of them had a project he wanted to get financing for, he would agree to vote for the pet projects proposed by the others in return for their support of his.

In 1946, Brown retired from the active management of GM, although he stayed on as a member of the board of directors until 1959. He set up the Broseco Corporation as a family enterprise, specializing in oil stocks, and he changed a large part of his holdings into Gulf Oil stock, becoming a member of the board of directors of the latter company and, in addition, a member of its finance and executive committees. He made a number of major conceptual and managerial contributions to Gulf before he retired from the company in 1956 to devote his full time to the Broseco Corporation. During these years, he also served as a director of several other companies and a member of the board of trustees of Johns Hopkins University. He died after a short illness on October 2, 1965 at the age of 80.

I believe that Don Brown's story will be both instructive and inspiring to managers today, when companies are gradually turning from the search for organization men to the search for executives with more creativity. Although the kind of opportunities Brown seized may not be available today, there are others that are just as good or better, if only the managers have the ability to recognize them. As Brown himself observed toward the end of his life, "It is still possible to make a fortune with an original brain."

ERNEST DALE

Wharton School
University of Pennsylvania
Philadelphia, Pa. 19104

Some Reminiscences of an Industrialist

Foreword

For some years I have been urged by members of my family to write a personal account of my experience in business. I have been very reluctant to do so. My reluctance was due, in part, to a natural fear that such an account would make it appear I was claiming personal credit for the accomplishments recited. Actually, they resulted from group activities, rather than from any individual or personal exploit. The great majority of important developments in American industry, especially in what is called "big business," necessarily are the product of cooperative effort by many men, joined together in mutual endeavor. Thinking in terms of "group effort" eventually becomes almost second nature to the matured business executive.

Recently, however, I was urged again to write the account by someone outside the family, and on a different basis. A friend reminded me that my active career with E. I. duPont de Nemours & Co., and with General Motors Corporation, covered a period of about 40 years, ending in 1946. He suggested that a detailed record of some of the significant events in which I was associated could serve a useful purpose as a sort of first-hand footnote to the history of industrial management in this country during the first half of the century.

This suggestion I found challenging, as something that might prove enlightening to my children. The period was one of marked evolutionary changes in concepts of industrial management, and one in which was forged the structure of America's economy as we know it today. To meet the needs of a society enjoying a constantly higher standard of living, rapid expansion took place in the mass production and distribution of goods. The economic forces attendant upon this growth led to the concentration of capital in relatively large units of industry. Fortunately, effective restraints were imposed by government to prevent resort to cartels; a truly competitive economy was preserved.

Lacking cartelization, what emerged was the development on a vast scale of corporate activity — a uniquely American and remarkably successful method for the employment of private capital in a free, competitive system.

It was this development which transformed American capitalism into a dynamic system, very different from the capitalism still prevalent in Europe. Ours became, in fact, a "people's capitalism," with public ownership, through large corporations, of private property. The wide dispersion of corporate ownership evolved from the general desire of Americans to share in the future of American business. Thus "big business" became the private concern of a multitude of people. And through this evolutionary process, the management of large corporations came to be akin, in a sense, to the exercise of a public trust.

The benefits which this system confers upon society are generally recognized. But little thought is given to the fundamental principles of industrial operation which make it possible, and still less to the process by which these principles were developed. Yet their evolution was, in many respects, one of the most significant features of our industrial history. For example, with the growth of large industrial organizations, it became necessary to devise techniques for more efficient internal control of operations. Competition demanded it. At the same time, and for the same reason, it was imperative to provide opportunity and incentive to employees at all levels of management for the full exercise of initiative and ingenuity. These were apparently conflicting requirements, with the fulfillment of both being essential to success. Yet over a period of years, they were satisfactorily resolved; first, by establishing realistic procedures for the measurement of performance by all operating units, and then by decentralizing management responsibilities to the fullest extent possible. Top level management provided the broad, coordinated policies necessary for general direction.

The gradual, progressive formulation of these fundamental policies was, of course, a critical achievement of the period, and in this, too, I was privileged to play a part. The basic purpose of management is to serve the interests of the owners of business, whom management directly represents. The performance of this function must take into account a wide range of phases, such as finance, technology, design and manufacture of products, pricing, distribution and sale of products, and personnel relations. But these cannot be treated entirely as separate and unrelated issues; each involves consideration of the others, and all of them are closely related to the broadest concepts of industrial operation. To truly serve the long-range interests of the owners of business, these basic concepts must recognize that the sound solution of problems embraced in each of the phases is of continuing and serious importance to the national economy. Always, too, there must be regard for the "dignity and worth of the individual," as it has been aptly stated. A reflection of these concepts in fundamental policy is essential because there is always an element of selfishness in the human breast, and in the absence of "enlightened self-interest" it is sometimes hard for an individual to recognize limitations on the particular phase of operation in which he is immediately involved. The limitations must be imposed by the coordinated policies of top management.

As corporations grew in size and in number, such considerations gradually shaped the basic policies of industrial management. There emerged during this period an awareness by enlightened leaders in industry of the absolute interdependence between the welfare of business and the common welfare of society. This became the first principle; the fundamental concept which informed and modified every major decision in the evolution of events.

This book seeks to recall and record some of those decisions and events. Perhaps it will help to illuminate, in a small way, the conditions and the industrial thinking which produced them, and also something of the impact they had on the welfare of our country. At any rate, that is the reason I have written this account, and arranged a private printing of it for my family and a few intimate friends.

I have included in the Appendix some materials which may usefully supplement in detail some of the incidents related in the text. In the chronicle itself are some recollections of my earlier life, and certain references to my family background. These should not be construed as an attempt at autobiography or personal memoirs; this is not intended in any sense. Certain episodes from my early years are mentioned to reflect something of my native traits and characteristics, and to record experiences with people in all walks of life, through boyhood and later, when I was engaged in direct fields of selling. Some understanding of human nature is important to anyone concerned with serving society, and the early experiences touched upon were invaluable to me.

I wish to emphasize here also the fact, which I hope is apparent throughout the text, that my observations are merely those of one who was privileged to associate with some of the great industrial leaders of our time, and who participated with them in the formulation of management policies. Sometimes I initiated original concepts; always, I tried to help bring about an understanding and acceptance, among employees, of the policies which were adopted by management. But the credit for the accomplishment of these things cannot be claimed by me. I never had administrative authority, outside of my immediate field of activities, except during the period 1937-1946, when the General Motors by-laws provided that the duties of the Chairman of the Board devolved upon me in his absence. At that time the Chairman was chief executive officer of the Corporation, and I was the Vice Chairman of the Board.

Comment on one other point seems to be in order here, inasmuch as it is not dealt with elsewhere. In suggesting this account, my friend urged me to describe the conditions and circumstances which made it possible for me, with no more than normal mental capacity, to accumulate a fairly sizeable fortune in the course of my career. He was mindful, as we all must be, of the fact that opportunities such as I enjoyed no longer are open to an individual employed in business undertakings. Today's high level of taxes limits severely the progressive investment of accumulated savings; hence opportunities which, in the early days of the century and before, were open to the individual, have been greatly impaired.

As set forth in the narrative, in 1918 I was elected Treasurer of the duPont Company, and to the Board of Directors and Executive Committee. I was thus privileged to share in the well-known stock bonus plan of that company until 1921, when I went to General Motors. On entering GM, I was elected to the Board, appointed a member of the Finance Committee, and made Vice President in charge of finance. I was therefore eligible to participate in the bonus plan which GM had inaugurated in 1919. During the years prior to the enactment of the present high income taxes, I was able also to save a large portion of my annual income for investment purposes. I have never had much experience with stock market dealings; in fact, during all those years I rarely looked at the stock quotations in the daily papers, and was content to invest accumulated savings chiefly in the company which employed me. On one occasion, in the mid-20's, I borrowed a substantial sum from my bank, against future income, to buy a block of General Motors stock. In addition, I was among a selected group of General Motors executives who were accorded the privilege in 1923 of buying a large block of GM stock from the duPont Company on a deferred installment plan. (The circumstances under which the duPont Company had acquired the stock on enforced purchase are related in my narrative.)

Doubtless my determination to invest as much as possible in the company with which I was employed had been influenced by my association as a young man with executives of the duPont Company. They always have been firm believers in the principle of "owner-management"; this was but natural, since the top management of the company from its earliest days had comprised individuals who themselves were very important stockholders. Unquestionably any enterprise benefits when its managers share in ownership. I believe the great accomplishments of the duPont Company can be attributed in no small degree to that happy management relationship.

The present restrictive laws militating against the accumulation of savings for investment apply particularly to salaried employees of industry, and render the progressive development of "owner-managers" virtually impossible. Yet opportunities continue to exist for individual initiative in manufacture and in productive endeavors of many kinds faced with the economic forces of competition. New products of research and technology continuously create new frontiers for productive enterprise.

There still remains, too, and I think always will, a great need for enterprise and initiative among dealers and merchants of all kinds in the conveyance of industry's products into the hands of the ultimate consumers. The vast array of entrepreneurs carrying on in these areas, as well as those engaged in primary supply, represent the "small businesss" upon which our national economy is so greatly dependent. Opportunities abide on all sides, and to the successful are available the rewards to which they are entitled.

In concluding this introduction, I would like to extend my thanks and appreciation to John W. Gibbons, of Silver Spring, Maryland, who has been most helpful in the editing and publication of the manuscript.

— DONALDSON BROWN

Port Deposit, Maryland
October, 1957

CHAPTER I

Background – Boyhood and College

I was born in Baltimore, Maryland, on February 1, 1885, the son of J. Willcox Brown and Ellen Turner Macfarland Brown. A twin sister died in infancy; we were the 11th and 12th children in the family. Two years later the 13th child, a daughter, was born. When I was seven years old, Hamilton, the oldest child, was killed in a driving accident. In the same year, a sister nine years older than I died from pneumonia contracted during an influenza epidemic in Baltimore.

My parents were Virginians. Father was born in Petersburg, Virginia, in 1833, the second of three sons of John Thompson Brown, a Princeton graduate and a man of marked literary talent. This grandfather, a practicing attorney in Petersburg, was a representative of Harrison County to the Virginia House of Delegates. He died at the untimely age of 34, when my father was only three years old.

In 1833, John Thompson Brown, moved apparently by some premonition, wrote and put into his wife's hands a letter to his sons, Henry and John, which was delivered to them after his death. Written in beautiful prose, replete with wise and wholesome counsel, this letter was preserved by the family, and later was published privately in booklet form under the title, "A Letter From a Father To His Sons." It is an inspiring document, combining lofty ideals with a wealth of practical good sense, and it has been a most salutary influence in the lives of all the descendants of John Thompson Brown. I believe it will continue to be. The letter is therefore reprinted in the Appendix of this volume, and I commend it most earnestly to the thoughtful attention of succeeding generations in the family.

Following the death of Mr. Brown in 1836, my grandmother returned with her three boys to the home of her parents, Mr. and Mrs. John Vaughan Willcox, in Petersburg. The family was in comfortable financial circumstances — Mr. Willcox was one of the wealthiest citizens of Virginia at the time — so that my father received a well-rounded education in arts and literature. He was graduated from the University of Virginia, and traveled extensively in Europe, where he undertook special studies in literature and history.

At the outbreak of the civil war, my father, living in Petersburg, took an active part in organizing a troop of volunteers, and during the war was promoted to the rank of colonel in the Ordnance Department of the Confederate Army. A series of illnesses prevented him from reaching military combat, but he nevertheless achieved an excellent record in behalf of the Confederate cause, which was dear to his heart.

My mother, Ellen Turner Macfarland Brown, was born in 1846, in Richmond, the daughter of Mr. and Mrs. William H. Macfarland. Thus she was 13 years younger than Father, whom she married in 1866. The Macfarlands lived in a spacious Richmond home which, in later years, was taken over as the home of the Westmoreland Club. Mr. Macfarland for many years was president of the Farmers' Bank of Richmond. Recently I came across a brochure published by the successor institution, which was created by the merger of several Virginia banks, and was interested to find, in the historical section, marked tributes to the character of William Macfarland, and reference to the deep concern which he held for the civic affairs of the community.

A man of considerable wealth in the ante-bellum days, Mr. Macfarland acquired early in the 19th century a tract of 4,000 acres in what is now Greenbrier County, West Virginia. There he established Glencoe, a summer home for the family, which was destined to play an important part in my own boyhood life. The Macfarlands spent much time at Glencoe, during suitable seasons of the year, traveling back and forth to Richmond by stagecoach.

As was the case with most wealthy citizens of the confederacy, my grandfather lost almost everything in the civil war. But he managed to retain the home in Greenbrier County, which became a haven for many members of the family in succeeding generations. With my brothers and sisters, I spent nearly all of my childhood summers at this plantation retreat.

Mrs. Macfarland was widowed for many years, but continued down to the time of her death to preside as the *grande dame* of Glencoe each summer. On the land were numerous houses which had been turned over to the families and descendants of those who had served as slaves. Through all the years afterwards, these Negro people displayed marked loyalty and respect to my grandmother, and to the Macfarland descendants and relatives.

Mr. Macfarland had been a pillar of St. Paul's Church, in Richmond, and his widow continued to exemplify the full meaning of his Christian beliefs. It was her regular custom to conduct prayers and services at her Glencoe home, which all the Negro retainers were urged to attend each Sunday evening. The services usually included the singing of hymns and spirituals by the Negroes present. A few hundred yards from Glencoe house, on the side of the driveway entrance, there was a small but very attractive chapel, where visiting clergy would conduct more formal services. The community always was invited to these services also. These religious ministrations unquestionably had profound influence on all who were brought into contact with the Christian beliefs of Mrs. Macfarland. And of course they were beliefs which her daughter — my mother — shared deeply.

During the years just before the turn of the century, my brother Thompson, a cousin, Francis Donaldson, and I were inseparable companions. Thompson was two and a half years older than I, and Francis was older than he, but the disparity in ages didn't interfere with our companion-

GLENCOE, IN GREENBRIER COUNTY, WEST VIRGINIA

ship. I, at least, refused to concede that I couldn't keep up with the activities of the older boys. All of us accepted as playmates the Negro sons of the families who were retainers on the Glencoe estate. These Negro boys regarded us as superiors, and were respectful towards us, but with it all we played together, and went hunting and fishing together, as bosom friends.

Often we white boys would go off on camping expeditions, usually to fish, taking one or more of the colored boys along as cook and general helper. The camping excursions usually were made on foot, with a pack horse to carry tent, provisions and supplementary equipment. On one such expedition we aimed at a spot in the mountains 53 miles away, where, we had been told, was wonderful fishing ground. I was 13 years old that summer. On the first day of the journey we covered about 40 miles.

During the afternoon, we came across a survey crew, with horses, which was headed in the same direction. Several times one or another of the surveyors, noticing my tender years and extreme fatigue, tried to persuade me to mount one of their horses and rest my legs. But my youthful pride would not permit me to give in. When at last we came to a stopping point for the night, and a campfire had been built, I sat down — and was unable to rise again to my feet! Next morning, however, just as determined as ever, I found myself restored sufficiently to carry on the remaining 13 miles.

The trout stream, when we arrived, was so swollen from recent rains that fishing was out of the question. We camped two or three days, hoping conditions would improve, but without any fish or game, provisions began to run short, and we had to start back home. Traveling on half empty stomachs, we made the 53 miles to Glencoe in two interminable days.

Many such expeditions enlivened the summer months at the country retreat. Pleasant to recall now, they were at the time often grueling experiences. If space permitted, much could be written of summer life while "comfortably" ensconsed at Glencoe. Perhaps mention of one incident is justified, as an example. On one camping trip during rainy weather, we placed our shoes one night in front of the campfire to dry them out. The following morning I found one of mine burned to a crisp, and it was necessary to improvise a foot wrapping for the 20 to 25-mile walk back home. I suffered a severe stone bruise which festered into a full-fledged boil on the ball of my foot. One day my sister, Fanny, undertook to drive me by horse and buggy to our family doctor, five miles from Glencoe. Approaching his house, we saw the good doctor working in a corn field, and called to him. The doctor examined my foot, decided surgery was required, and taking a knife from his pocket proceeded to take care of the situation on the spot. Fanny contributed some of her wearing apparel for bandaging and we went back home. The injury healed in a few days.

The mountains of West Virginia must have been providentially free of germs in those days!

During the winter months I attended public schools near our Baltimore home at 110 West North Avenue, which in my boyhood years was at the northern boundary of the city. As in the summer, my brother Thompson and I were inseparable companions. We became interested in electrical apparatus, and spent a great deal of time experimenting. Along with a few of our neighborhood friends, we formed in 1895 what we called the Taney Place Electric Company. (The area for a couple of blocks along North Avenue was named Taney Place for a parkway along the center.) "Headquarters" of the company were established in our basement. Soon we had telegraph connections with the third floor of the house, where our bedroom was situated. From a General Gray, a friend of Father, we also acquired telautograph instruments, then still in the experimental stage, and these were similarly arranged to convey written messages back and forth.

Father was much interested in our activities, and, I guess, like all good fathers, a little proud, too, because he showed no hesitancy in telling his friends and business associates all about it. One of these was Fred Todd, the manager of the Baltimore office of the General Electric Company. The result was a challenge to the Taney Place Electric Company from Mr. Todd; he offered a silver cup, duly inscribed, as a prize to the boy in the company who, within a certain number of months, came up with the best invention of a new application of electricity.

I won the prize. Mr. Todd himself judged the entries. Mine was a device which registered, at a remote location, which of three denominations of coins was dropped into a slot at the other end of the electrical hook-up. I must have known something of the coin devices, which were then in limited use; nevertheless, my apparatus, which actually worked, was counted as an "invention."

My parents had not always lived in Baltimore. After their marriage, Father went into the banking business in Richmond as a partner in a well-known private firm. He had no business or banking experience, and the firm failed during the national crisis in 1873. Later, moving to Baltimore, he re-entered the banking business, again to suffer defeat. With this second failure, in 1893, the home in Baltimore was forced to virtually close down, Mother remaining with Father there to help him patch up the broken pieces of his career, the rest of us moving into the home of a cousin, Mrs. Nancy von Ahlfeldt, at Union, West Virginia. Cousin Nancy happened to be in Europe for the winter, and with generous spirit made her home, "Walnut Grove," complete with its staff of servants, available to the younger children in the Brown family.

Thompson and I continued our studies that winter under the tutelage of an older sister. When summer came, we children went to Glencoe, as usual, for the summer season.

Meanwhile, in Baltimore, conditions improved. Happily for the family, the integrity of Father's character had been recognized by important interests concerned with banking activities in Baltimore, and he was invited to accept the presidency of the Maryland Trust Company. In the fall of 1894, the West North Avenue home was reopened, and we children returned to public school.

My father served as president of the trust company for 10 years. During this period, he became interested in the promotion of a small railroad system in Mexico, and the trust company extended loans for initial construction, having had assurances from other interests, including some in Britain, that basic capital requirements would be forthcoming. The capital was not supplied, and through default on outstanding obligations of the Mexican railroad company, the Maryland Trust Company was forced into receivership in 1903. (Years later, the railroad was built and is now operating as the Vera Cruz and Pacific Railroad.)

This third failure led to my father's final retirement, in a penniless state. Just the year before, my oldest sister, Mary, had married John M. Glenn, a prominent citizen of Baltimore, and a man of some financial means. John gave much-needed financial assistance to my mother and father; more importantly, he gave counsel and advice which proved of great moral encouragement to Father, and contributed to his peace of mind and enjoyment of life in his remaining years.

My parents gave up the Baltimore home and moved to Albemarle County, Virginia, where they made their home with an older sister of mine, Nannie, and her husband, Guy Corbett, who was engaged in orcharding on a small scale. Father had suffered a heart condition for some years, but it did not disturb him greatly during the 10 years of his retirement. He gained pleasure in odd jobs around the outer grounds, and took much pride in the care of shrubbery and flowers. He and mother occupied a cottage, but took their meals with the Corbett family. Near by was the home of Mr. Chiswell D. ("Chilly") Langhorne, and the "Langhorne Daughters," who were models for Charles Dana Gibson, a son-in-law, in portraying the famous "Gibson Girls." My father had known Mr. Langhorne quite intimately in earlier years, and the association between them, and between the families, became most pleasant and gratifying on both sides through succeeding years.

The end came for Father in 1913. He was found dead in his bed, and apparently had passed away in his sleep without regaining consciousness. His body was taken to Baltimore for interment in Greenmount Cemetery, where his deceased children were at rest. I was living in Wilmington at the time, and went to Baltimore to make the arrangements. I have the most gratifying memory of the deep respect for Father evidenced by his former associates on whom I called, and their hearty willingness to serve as honorary pallbearers.

The observant reader already may have noted how the numeral "3" seemed to loom so large in my father's life. He was born in 1833, one of three sons. He was married at the age of 33, his bride being 13 years younger than he, and they had 13 children. Father suffered three business failures; in 1873, 1893, and 1903. His death came in 1913. A most curious repetition of coincidence.

In the fall of 1898, five years before the home in Baltimore was broken up, Thompson and I were admitted to Virginia Polytechnic Institute. At age 13, I was unduly young, but apparently Father sensed that time was running out in which he could afford to provide the education he desired for me. I don't know how he managed to obtain my admission — doubtless some wires were pulled — but I completed the freshman year on the honor roll, working very hard. At Glencoe the next summer I came down with typhoid fever, which was more or less an annual event among the younger folk there. Like the others, I received the standard treatment of cold baths and quiet; I managed to recover in time for the opening of the fall term at V.P.I. That September, our older sister, Fanny, came to visit Thompson and me — we were both studying electrical engineering — and gave me an "older sister" lecture on the importance of not working too hard. I took her lecture to heart. For two years I refrained so assiduously from working hard that I failed numerous examinations, and entered the senior year with several studies to make up. An older cousin in the same class had a scholastic record matching mine very closely. Early in the fall term, during a jovial session with classmates, I offered to bet my cousin that I would graduate when the next commencement arrived. He took me up, the wager involving his own graduation also. I don't remember ever collecting the five dollars, but I did settle down to work, and at the appointed time I received a degree of Bachelor of Science in electrical engineering. It took my cousin two more years to finish.

Father then sent Thompson and me to Cornell for a postgraduate course. I was then 17. We completed a year's work with passing marks, but there remained two or three courses, languages, I think, which would have to be made up before securing a Cornell degree. We planned to make them up in three or four months of the following year. Before the fall term opened, Father had suffered his final business failure, and college days were over. Thompson and I went to work.

CHAPTER II

Beginnings of a Business Career

One of life's most pleasant "miracles," which a young man takes in stride, is the sudden creation of a new and completely different kind of world. In 1903, such a change occurred for me. I left behind me the memories of classrooms and boyhood play, of summer-long vacations and the security of the family home. Almost overnight that world disappeared. In its place was the challenging future of life in an adult world; the stirring prospect of new adventures and of great opportunities.

Thompson found employment with the duPont Company. I went to work in Baltimore at a drafting board for the Baltimore & Ohio Railroad. But I remained there only a few months. Soon I was attracted to a selling job for the Sprague Electric Company. (Not to be confused with the present-day company of the same name.) It was a subsidiary of General Electric Company, although the ownership was not generally known at the time. The opportunity came to me through Mr. Todd, Baltimore office manager of General Electric; the same Mr. Todd who had offered the prize some years before to boys in the Taney Place Electric Company. Of such strands is the pattern of one's life woven.

I was sent to Bloomfield, New Jersey, where I spent several months in the Sprague Company's factory, learning from work at the bench, and from observations, as much as possible about the equipment and apparatus which I would be expected to sell. Early in 1904 I returned to Baltimore with the impressive title of Manager of the Baltimore Sales Office, my territory embracing all of Maryland and part of Virginia. I was 19 years old that February, and was extremely fortunate to be received into the home of my sister Mary and her husband, John M. Glenn, who treated me as if I were their own son.

Less than a month later, on a Sunday morning, came the tragic Baltimore fire of 1904, which destroyed most of the city's business district, including the principal newspapers, numerous banks and office buildings. My office on one of the top floors of the Maryland Trust Building contained a supply of small electric motors used for display purposes. I went to the building, hoping to remove them, but the fire by then was unmanageable and the motors were destroyed.

Baltimore's reconstruction created an immediate demand for electric motors and flexible wire cable, products of the Sprague Company. The latter item carried the trade name "Greenfield Cable," with patent rights controlled exclusively by Sprague. Over the course of several months, I gained and maintained contact with several local architects engaged in planning the reconstruction of buildings. Naturally, I pointed out to them the virtues of specifications calling for the use of "Greenfield Cable" in wiring installations.

Meanwhile, the New York headquarters of the company had made encouraging progress in the use of individual electric motors to power the presses and other equipment in printing establishments, replacing the older system of line-belts operating off of shaft-driven, centrally situated motors. So I made contact with some of the printing establishments, and arranged for company representatives from New York to explain the advantages of the individual power equipment. We succeeded in gaining the interest of both the SUN papers and the Baltimore NEWS.

Then, on a day that was memorable in my young mind, I was called by Mr. Todd to his office, where I found with him the salesman in charge of small GE motors. I was given to understand that I had been unduly ambitious in pushing the sale of Sprague equipment in competition with the "more suitable rights" of General Electric to serve the needs of reconstruction in Baltimore. As I said above, the Sprague Company was an "unrecognized" subsidiary of

GE. Moreover, it was through Mr. Todd that I had obtained employment with the company. Hence, I did not feel I was in a position to object. But I had the unpleasant sensation that my wings had been clipped. Certainly I didn't relish being encouraged by my bosses to be "less aggressive." I continued on the job until the fall of 1907, but was not too happy, and was alert to any other opportunities which might present themselves.

In the spring of 1907 an opportunity did arise which to my immature judgment seemed very attractive. It was the promotion of a patented device for transporting coal, pulp wood and similar products in tram cars, operated on suspended wire cables. They would serve to link mines and forests with main railroad lines, obviating the need for expensive construction of spur tracks or subsidiary lines.

My connection with this enterprise came about purely by chance. In 1905, I had been invited to join a group of six or seven young men in sharing a summer establishment on a hill on the outskirts of Baltimore. All were older than I, and most were young lawyers just starting in practice. We were a congenial crowd, summering in a bachelor establishment which some of the neighbors dubbed "Stagger Inn." One of the young lawyers with whom I became especially friendly got interested in the tramway patent through associations in his law practice. I was somewhat familiar with the rugged mountain country of West Virginia, and my lawyer friend sold me on the idea of taking over the patent rights on the device for that state.

I succeeded in interesting Dabney Davis, a prominent lawyer in Charleston, West Virginia, who was active in various coal mining operations. After consulting a close friend of his, Harry Frazier, former chief engineer for the Chesapeake & Ohio Railroad, who told him the equipment was feasible for the purpose intended, Mr. Davis agreed to accept the presidency of a company to be formed.

I had no money to invest and the immediate family couldn't help me out, so I went to see a first cousin, Hamilton Barksdale, the general manager of the duPont Company. He loaned me enough money to get started. It was not intended as capital necessary to establish the company — only a couple of thousand dollars — but money to cover my expenses in getting the project organized. I counted on Mr. Frazier's endorsement, and Mr. Davis' prominence, to attract a nucleus of capital through stock subscriptions among their friends. I imagined that additional financing then could be obtained by issuance of securities of some sort. I expected a personal participation in stock of the company in consideration of a "finder's fee." Thus, was the West Virginia Aerial Tramway Company set up in Charleston, with Mr. Davis as president and with headquarters in his law office.

Up to this point, I had kept my salaried position with the Sprague Company, but in the fall of 1907 I decided to cut loose, and moved to Charleston in an attempt to expedite the undertaking. I spent several months contacting possible users of the equipment, and working on engineering designs of the towers, cable sizes and power equipment that would be needed.

But the time came when the raising of capital began to look questionable. I was running short of money myself, and was unwilling, in view of the uncertain situation, to borrow more. To save expenses, I moved in with my sister and her husband, the Corbetts of Albemarle County, Virginia. The headquarters of the parent company promoting the transportation system was in Roanoke, Virginia, not far away, so I made occasional visits to check on progress. Gradually, I began to sense many practical difficulties in the design, as well as the difficulty, if not impossibility, of raising sufficient capital for my West Virginia venture. In the mid-summer of 1908 I gave up hope, and reported the facts of the case to Mr. Barksdale.

It happened that Mr. Barksdale at the time was considering investment in a newly-designed power drill for use in mining, quarrying and heavy construction. He suggested that I investigate it, with the understanding that if he decided the drill had economic value he would back me with a working interest in its exploitation. I spent a few weeks with the inventor, watching the drill in operation in various places. But I found myself forced to recommend against the commercial value of the equipment, and further studies were suspended.

Mr. Barksdale next suggested the possibility of a job with the duPont Company. He put me in touch with people in the Sales Department, who offered me an opportunity to sell explosives. I accepted. My first assignment was to go through a course in one of the central laboratories, to learn something about the characteristics of explosives. After two or three months, I was transferred to the Technical Division of the Sales Department, to familiarize myself with the economic uses of explosives in various fields of application. I was sent first to Hazelton, Pennsylvania, where one of the "old hands" was demonstrating the use of explosives in anthracite coal mines. After a couple of months with him, I went out on my own in demonstrations in quarry work, at the New York Aqueduct, then under construction, in soft coal mining and in agricultural applications. This basic training over, I was then counted as ready for the sales force.

My first actual selling job with the company was in the Contractors' Division, under the capable direction of Ed Ferriday. That began in 1909, and I remained under his direction for two or three years. One incident during that period occurred in Jackson, Breathet County, Kentucky. Perhaps it sticks in my memory because it illustrated so well the rough-and-ready type of social order which still existed in that part of the country well into the present century.

The Lane Construction Company had a contract to build a new railroad from a terminus at Jackson to a newly-opened coal field in West Virginia. My job was to sell the company the explosives it would need. In the course of my duties I made an early trip to Jackson with Mr. Lane himself. The town having no hotel facilities, two farm houses were being used for lodgings. One, near the railroad, housed Mr. Lane and his company officials. The other, a half-mile or so across town, was turned over to the salesmen, like myself, who were flocking into the community.

I spent the greater part of one day with Mr. Lane and his people, and succeeded in getting a contract signed for total explosives requirements. I stayed with them for supper, and then started off on foot for my own lodgings. It was election day, and I had to push my way through numerous groups of noisy celebrants, all much the worse for moonshine liquor. At my "hotel," I found a group assembled in an improvised lobby, listening to a discourse by a retired judge. He was describing some of his experiences in the local court, with particular reference to a notorious character named "Bad Jake" Noble, who was highly proficient in the art of disposing unlawfully of political enemies. A member of Noble's gang, it seems, had been imprisoned in Jackson only a few days before.

Suddenly the speaker was interrupted by a great hue and cry outside the "hotel." The town jailer had been killed, his prisoner released. We all rushed over to the nearby jail, just in time to watch "Bad Jake" Noble ride quietly out of town on horseback. Nobody followed him; no authority was willing to take any action against him at all. On return visits to Jackson, I was told that Noble continued to range through the surrounding hills, unmolested by police.

Another more significant incident had to do with the sale of explosives to the Langhorne Construction Company, which had obtained a contract to build 90 miles of railroad for the Consolidation Coal Company. It is likely that I got the assignment because of the long friendship between the Chiswell Langhorne family and my own; at any rate, the head of the construction company was Allan Langhorne, a cousin of "Chilly." I had several preliminary meetings with him, and then arranged for a conference in the Huntington, West Virginia office of the duPont Company. The servicing of continuous needs would be under the jurisdiction of that office, with Charles W. Phellis in charge, and I wanted to get the benefit of his knowledge and experience in getting the contract signed with a man who was acknowledged to be a "tough customer."

Mr. Phellis and I both had been informed by Mr. Langhorne that he had been quoted a lower price on blasting powder than ours, and we had tried unsuccessfully to persuade the home office in Wilmington to back down from the rigid price given us. Our conference began in a friendly atmosphere. Then we got around to black powder, and Mr. Langhorne showed us a letter in which a competitor quoted it at $1.05 per keg, compared with our price of $1.10. When he discovered that we were unable to cut our price to match the other offer, Mr. Langhorne went into a rage such as I have never seen in my life. He shouted and raged. He had been urged by the Consolidation Coal Company to place his explosives business with the duPont Company. He had signed the railroad construction contract on the assumption, however, that he would not be restricted in any way in the procurement of supplies. Mr. Langhorne was trembling with anger. He was not going to be held up, nobody was going to point a gun at his head, and tell him who he had to do business with. He stamped out of the office.

Unwilling to accept defeat, I rushed out after Mr. Langhorne, catching him before he got into an elevator. I talked with him a few minutes, got him settled down to the extent that he was willing to go back into the office. There the two of us had a quiet talk; I pointed out the advantage of buying his blasting powder from the same source as his other explosives. I reminded him of the consistently high quality of the duPont products, and of the company's excellent reputation for follow-up customer service. To make a long sales story short, I finally got him to agree, called Mr. Phellis back into the office, and in a few minutes the contract was signed.

Afterwards, I went to Wilmington and told the whole story to my boss, Ed Ferriday. I urged that in view of the lower price quoted by a dependable competitor, we should voluntarily match that price, even though the contract at the higher figure already had been signed. Mr. Ferriday agreed, and we appeared before the general sales manager of the company to plead our case. We couldn't get him to budge an inch; the price was $1.10, it was going to stay there, and stay it did, throughout the entire construction job.

I have always felt that the general sales manager didn't believe me when I assured him I had not given Mr. Langhorne any intimation that I would try to get the contract price reduced. But that was the case, and I never had any further explanations to make.

The Consolidation Coal Company had urged the contractor to place his explosives business with the duPont Company at the suggestion of Ed Ferriday. His appeal was on the basis of reciprocity; the duPont Company was an important customer of the coal company. The sharp clash with Allan Langhorne made a deep impression on me. It must have contributed toward a fundamental concept which I came later to accept. At any rate, the fact is that in subsequent years, after joining General Motors, I opposed consistently any resort to reciprocity in trade relations, and GM adopted a firm policy in accord with that viewpoint.

In 1911 several men left the duPont Company to join a newly-created competitive black powder company. Among them was a very effective salesman in the Pittsburgh area, whose territory of four counties embraced important mining and quarrying activities requiring large consumption of black blasting powder. It was feared this salesman's defection to a competitive producer would lead to a substantial diversion of business.

I was chosen to replace this particular salesman. Accordingly, I was transferred from the Contractors' Division and took up residence in a boarding house in Phillipsburgh. There were virtually no automobiles in those days by which to cover a very large territory. Travel was by train to local stops, then by horse and buggy through the surrounding area to the customers. Once a month or so I went to Pittsburgh for consultations and guidance. The duPont Company's excellent reputation for quality product and good customer service made it possible for me to hold on to the business in that area during my assignment, which extended over approximately 18 months.

I left the Sales Department in 1912 when Mr. Barksdale, the general manager of the company, invited me to join his office staff. As previously related, I had turned to Mr. Barksdale for financial help in my unsuccessful attempt to launch the West Virginia tramway company. Then I had investigated the drilling equipment in which he was interested, after which he had been instrumental in gaining employment for me in direct selling. I was greatly surprised to receive the offer of a transfer to his own office. In succeeding years, looking back on 1912, I continued to be surprised that Mr. Barksdale would be willing to take a young cousin under his cloak. However, in fairness to both of us, and with due modesty and a regard for accuracy, I must concede that my service in the Contractors' Division, as well as in the Sales Department, if not spectacular, had at least been of a satisfactory caliber.

Mr. Barksdale had a private secretary and an adequate office staff; my assignment was to attend to analytical work. This brought me into contact with all the departments under his jurisdiction, and particularly with the secretaries and assistants of department managers. In addition, I was called to sit in frequent group meetings of Mr. Barksdale and his department managers. This experience was invaluable; I came to learn something of management problems, and of the methods for attacking them as they arose.

In this way was the stage set for the next — and decisive — milestone of my business career.

CHAPTER III

R = T x P

An event occurred in 1914 which proved to be the turning point of my business career. The circumstances which led up to it were accidental, and I have often wondered what might have been my fate and fortune in industrial management if I had not, that summer, hit upon the mathematical equation which serves as the heading of this chapter.

Mr. Barksdale was in bad health and was forced to take extended time off, which he spent with his family in Westport, New York. During a period of such absence from the office, the President of the company, Coleman duPont, called for a study and report on the performance and accomplishments of the several operating departments. I undertook the job.

In due time I completed a report which apparently made a deep impression on Mr. duPont. He suggested to John J. Raskob, the Treasurer of the Company, that I belonged in the Financial Department, and Mr. Raskob agreed. I was glad to accept his offer of a transfer, and thus became Assistant Treasurer, in the Financial Department, with particular duties assigned in the field of analytical work.

The basis of my report gauging the performance of the various operating departments was a simple mathematical formula: $R = T \times P$. The factor R represented the rate of return on capital invested, which is a final and fundamental measure of industrial efficiency in terms of management's primary responsibility. The T stood for the rate of turnover of invested capital, and P for the percentage of profit on sales. On the investment side T was broken down into components, embracing plant and other fixed investment items, as well as amounts tied up in working capital in various categories such as raw materials, work in process, finished product, accounts receivable and required operating cash balances.

All investment items, severally, were reflected in terms of ratio to sales, and the reciprocal of the sum total of such ratios represented the rate of turnover (T). In turn, items of costs, broken down into significant categories, were reflected in each case as percentage of sales. The difference between the sum total of cost items and 100 percent represented, of course, the percentage profit on sales.

This approach resulted in a specific disclosure of causes and effects for the return on investment as shown for each department. Effective control, or the lack of it, for any item on either side of the equation could be identified, thus making possible efforts to improve conditions. The method of analysis also lent itself to measured calculations of the effect, in terms of stockholder benefits, of price reductions which might result in expanded sales volume.

A chart room was set up where these statistical data pertaining to each segment of the company's operations were displayed. Meetings were held regularly with department heads, and extended discussions were held regarding the possibility of improving specific cost and expense items, in relation to the end-result of return on invested capital. Such a chart room is still in effective use in the duPont Company. Needless to say, however, notable improvement has been made in the techniques of presentation since that pioneer undertaking of more than 40 years ago!

The chart room was under the jurisdiction of the Treasurer's Department. It continues to be. But that department never has had any administrative authority over operations. This distinction is basic and important. Under direction of the executive officer in charge of finance, economic data are collected and analyzed. The results are made available for consideration by all of the operating departments concerned, and frequently the recommendations following from the analyses are adopted as a matter of operating policy.

The same relationship exists in the matter of making forecasts, on which decisions must be based concerning purchases, production schedules, future capital requirements and prospective profits. Here again the economic analyses of the finance department are brought to bear on the formulation of policies necessary for coordinated control of company operations. The findings are made available to assist the operating heads of the several departments involved. Thus the work performs a vital role in industry. But it does not interfere with nor prevent the proper decentralization of management responsibilities, which is essential to a large industrial organization if it is to succeed in a competitive economy.

A few years after transferring to the Treasurer's Department, I brought into the staff a full-time political economist. His function was to provide consultation and advice on forward trends of the national economy which might be expected to affect future demand for the company's products. This made possible an informed testing of forecasts made by the operational division. It also provided useful guidance for many management decisions. Services of this kind have continued through the years, and the employment of economists is now a general practice among the larger units in American industry.

In 1914, with the outbreak in Europe of World War I, the duPont Company was called upon to supply explosives of various kinds to the Allies on an ever-ascending scale. New plants were built to meet the contracts, usually with advance payments to meet construction costs. The contracts with Allied countries, chiefly Britain and France, proved highly profitable, but justifiably so in view of the extreme hazards involved. The company found itself at times with large cash balances on hand, accumulated for construction purposes, and one of my duties in the Treasurer's office was to invest surplus cash in short-time securities. The return from these temporary investments proved to be of considerable consequence.

With the entry of our own country into the war, further expansion of plants was undertaken to meet the enlarged requirements of our own government, and the commercial operations of the company became, for awhile, relatively insignificant.

Meanwhile, following the outbreak of the European war, Coleman duPont, being in poor health, decided to retire from his arduous duties. He was succeeded in the presidency by Pierre duPont. At this time, Coleman sold his entire holdings of common stock to a company created for the purpose, the Christianna Securities Company. Part of the payment was made with funds raised through banking accommodations. Pierre duPont and other members of the family were the principal purchasers of the common stock of this newly-created holding company.

The duPonts, believing firmly in the efficacy of owner-management, extended participation in the common stock of Christianna Securities to top executives of the duPont Company, on the basis of borrowed money. This gave the top executives an important stake in the welfare of the company they were serving, and unquestionably was a contributing factor in the highly successful performance of the company during World War I and afterwards.

Among individual employees in the earlier days, one of importance to the company's success was Mr. Barksdale, the General Manager, to whom I referred earlier. Prior to World War I, the company was in the throes of extensive reorganization, in conformance with a Federal court dissolution decree. Certain plants and facilities were separated from duPont Company and transferred to two companies created for the purpose, Hercules Powder and Atlas Powder. The stock issued in each case was distributed to the stockholders of duPont Company. In addition to plant transfer, the staffing of the new companies by qualified executive personnel was required. Mr. Barksdale played an important role in this reorganization. Evidence of his highly constructive service to the company is the fact that during the great expansion which took place shortly after the reorganization, many top managerial positions in the two separated companies, as well as in duPont Company itself, were filled by highly competent men who had been trained under Mr. Barksdale.

In later years, I came across a paper by Dr. Henry Wriston in which, describing the basic American principles encouraging private, individual initiative, he used an expression, "the dignity and worth of the individual." This phrase aptly describes the basic concept on which Mr. Barksdale's whole life in business administration was founded. Never did he yield, for expediency's sake, to the temptations of dictatorship. Always he strove to maintain freedom of opportunity for the individual; opportunity to progress through the display of initiative in coping with the problems at hand; and opportunity to qualify for ever-expanding responsibilities along the ladder of promotion.

Illustrative of Mr. Barksdale's constant regard for the welfare of the men in his charge was an incident which occurred while he was inspecting a dynamite plant in which nitro-glycerine was being made. This is an extremely hazardous process, requiring close controls to guard against explosion.

After finding everything in order, Mr. Barksdale asked the foreman in charge what he would do if the temperature in the mixing vat rose to a certain hazardous level. The foreman correctly described the procedure which would correct the situation without personal hazard.

"What would you do," Mr. Barksdale continued, "if it went higher than that — to an unmanageable level?"

The foreman's answer wasn't satisfactory.

"No, Dick," said Mr. Barksdale. "If you see the thermometer approaching that point, run just as fast as you can and get behind that barricade over there which is intended for just such an emergency. We can rebuild the nitroglycerine plant. We cannot rebuild you."

Prior to the end of World War I, Pierre duPont and John Raskob became personally interested in General Motors Corporation, and in interests held by W. C. Durant, who during temporary separation from GM had formed the Chevrolet Motor Company. The separation occurred when GM, through financial reverses, had been taken over by a banking group, with control vested in a voting trust agreement. During this period, Charles W. Nash served as President. GM affairs had been straightened out during the interim, and when the trust agreement expired, Durant was brought back as President, largely through the influence of Pierre and Raskob. Pierre became Chairman of the Board and Raskob Chairman of the Finance Committee. Both had great belief in the future possibilities of the fledgling automotive industry, and they counted on Durant's imagination and competency to deal with the operating affairs involved.

This interest led the two men in 1917 to urge upon the duPont Company a substantial investment in GM common stock. As a result of the war-time operations, surplus cash had accumulated in the company beyond any foreseeable needs of its own business, and both men asserted that the investment of these resources in GM would better serve the interests of stockholders than would a dividend distribution.

On the Board and in the governing committees of the duPont Company were many who, at first, questioned the wisdom of such an investment. They questioned whether the company should invest cash not needed for its own business in another enterprise so far remote from the experience and skills of the organization serving the interests of the duPont Company stockholders. They suggested, instead, that the cash which could not be employed constructively in the business should be distributed to stockholders, thus being available to them individually for such investment as each might choose.

But Raskob persisted, and he was an effective salesman. It might be well to explain at this point how it happened that I came into intimate association with Raskob's activities leading to the duPont Company's initial investment in GM stock. The voting trust in control of GM, previously mentioned, was headed up by James A. Storrow, of the Lee Higenson & Co. Shortly before the expiration of the voting trust, in the course of routine contacts with bankers over the country in the interest of the duPont Company, I came into contact with Storrow in Boston. He knew of the interest of Raskob and Pierre duPont in GM affairs, and went to great length to picture the situation to me, with a request that I convey his views to those gentlemen. He expressed deep anxiety as to what would happen with the restoration of control to Durant and his associates.

Upon my return to Wilmington I laid the picture before Raskob and Pierre, finding both of them entirely satisfied with the way things were headed, and opposed to any perpetuation of control by what they called "the bankers." Later, Raskob kept me closely informed of his thinking on the question of investing duPont Company surplus cash in GM. (At the time I was not on the Board, nor a member of either of the governing committees, but I was serving as Assistant Treasurer under Raskob.) Raskob's most appealing argument for the investment by duPont was that the automobile industry had a great future, and that the ownership of GM stock by a large industrial concern would have a beneficial influence upon General Motors. The duPont Company investment would be under jurisdiction of the Finance Committee, with appropriate influence thus being exerted by individuals experienced in successful industrial financial policies.

There was never any thought on the part of the duPont Company or anyone in its management of attempting to participate in the operation of General Motors. It was clearly understood that the duPont interests would exercise responsibilities solely in the financial field, leaving the administrative affairs entirely in the hands of GM's own organization. This concept was strictly adhered to through the years. Responsibility in the duPont organization over its GM investment has rested with its Finance Committee; the Executive Committee has had no voice in it, nor has any other executive of the company, as such.

After numerous and extended debates, Raskob finally carried the day. The duPont Company in 1917 made an important investment in General Motors, which was enlarged in subsequent years. During the extended debates, one basic point of policy was settled, to the effect that while an investment in GM stock was sanctioned, it was only as concerned surplus cash in the treasury beyond what could reasonably be regarded as representing needs of the business. However, as related later in this chapter, a few years later the company was forced into an unwanted addition to its General Motors investment, resorting to bank borrowing for the purpose.

Some years ago, the U. S. Department of Justice brought action against the duPont Company, members of the duPont family, General Motors, and others, seeking to compel the duPont Company to dispose of its GM stock holdings. I will not go into details here regarding this. A long trial was held in the Federal District Court in Chicago, after which a decision was handed down by the Court giving a sweeping clearance to all parties concerned. The government appealed to the U. S. Supreme Court, which early in 1957, by a four to two vote, handed down a decision holding the duPont Company liable under the Clayton Act, and referring the case back to the District Court in Chicago. Under the Supreme Court's decision, General Motors is cleared, as are all other parties, and the declaration stands that holdings of GM stock by the duPont Company for *purely investment purposes* is legally sanctionable. As I write this, a few months after the decision was handed down, the matter has not yet reached the point of hearings before the court to which the case was remanded, and it is impossible to foresee how the necessities of the situation finally will be worked out.

In March, 1918, I was elected Treasurer of the duPont Company, succeeding Raskob, who was elected a Vice President. In that year Raskob began giving more and more of his time to GM affairs, and around the middle of the year, before the end of World War I, he retired from the Executive Committee. At his urging, I was elected a member of the duPont Board, and also a member of the Executive Committee to fill the vacancy caused by Raskob's retirement from that Committee. In 1919, I was named

duPONT EXECUTIVE COMMITTEE, shortly before the Armistice in 1918. L. to R., front row: F. L. Connable, H. G. Haskell, Irenee duPont (Chairman), H. F. Brown, Lammot duPont. Back row, Donaldson Brown, R. R. M. Carpenter, F. W. Pickard, William Coyne and F. G. Tallman.

also to membership on the Finance Committee, which has been retained up to the present day.

The armistice of November 11, 1918, ending World War I, marked a turning point for the duPont Company. In serving the needs of our allies, beginning in 1914, and during our own participation in the war, the company had made great additions to its existing plants and had built enormous new plants for the manufacture of smokeless powder and explosives of various kinds. While the plants themselves would be virtually useless for peace-time commercial purposes, the organization in the course of serving war-time needs had developed managerial skills and know-how in manufacturing operations. The Development Department, headed by Walter Carpenter, through this period gave continuing and very effective study to opportunities for future employment of capital and of proven personnel. Special attention was given to broadened fields related to the chemical industry, as distinct from the explosives business in which the company previously had been primarily engaged. The Development Department played a magnificent role in this post-war planning.

Of course, the Executive Committee (which was the "War-Time Executive Committee" for the duration) had a major part to play in the forward planning, with respect to policy considerations, as also did the Finance Committee. Almost immediately after the armistice, for example, the Executive Committee appointed a subcommittee, of which I was a member, to survey the personnel in executive and supervisory positions. This subcommittee was headed by H. Fletcher Brown (no relation). Through collaboration with top management, qualifications of personnel were catalogued, with careful notations of special skills. The lists were studied by the subcommittee to appraise the potentialities of each individual in various fields of management. Then they were reviewed from the standpoint of the new undertakings which were evolving from the work of the Development Department. The result was the listing of personnel in categories related to their potential utilization. The Executive Committee authorized the retention of all personnel in the lists for an extended period, during which there was opportunity to determine how to fit the maximum number into permanent employment. All department heads were furnished the listing of personnel, together with the findings of the subcommittee, which enabled them through transfers to meet their requirements in departmental forward planning.

Opportunities also existed in this period for many to transfer to General Motors, to fill gaps in managerial positions in that far-flung organization. Among these, two outstanding executives come immediately to mind. One was E. F. Johnson, who had demonstrated marked managerial ability as general manager of the Old Hickory Plant, which had been built solely for war-time production. E. F. would have been cordially welcome to remain in the duPont organization, but he elected to transfer to General Motors, where he and others similarly transferred performed with high credit.

The other outstanding individual was John L. Pratt, whom I consider as perhaps my closest friend and business associate over the years. Pratt had been working in the Explosives Division with Mr. Barksdale prior to the War. Mr. Barksdale died in 1918: at the time Pratt was on his staff, engaged in the development of future plans. He continued this activity, with particular responsibility for investigating the possibilities of the production of nitrogen from the air. The process which had been suggested involved large power requirements, and Pratt spent considerable time exploring the matter with Norwegian interests, and with Colonel Hugh L. Cooper, noted hydropower engineer, and others. The project was abandoned as not feasible. Pratt, like the others, found a future of highly constructive service in the General Motors organization.

As Treasurer of the duPont Company in this post-war period, I, too, consulted the list provided through the work of the H. F. Brown subcommittee. I wanted to bring someone into the Financial Department who had operating experience, and who therefore could be helpful in accomplishing the coordinated financial control with which I was deeply concerned. My first choice among those who had been temporarily left without assignment was F. B. Davis, who had been manager of the Carney's Point smokeless powder plant. But I couldn't sell him on the idea of entering into the work of the Financial Department. He became manager of the Arlington plant engaged in pyralin manufacture; later he went to GM for a time, and finally he became President of the U. S. Rubber Company. My second choice was Angus Echols, who went into the matter thoroughly and then accepted. Angus fitted into the pattern of the Department in a wonderful way. Later on, when Walter Carpenter became Treasurer, Angus served as his right-hand man, and in time he himself was elected Treasurer and member of the Executive Committee. Eventually when Walter assumed presidency of the company, Angus became Chairman of the Finance Committee.

During war years, as mentioned earlier, the duPont Company management was put into the hands of a "War-Time Executive Committee," consisting of top executives functioning largely in a collective manner. As the war drew to a close, Irenee duPont, Chairman of the Executive Committee, appointed a subcommittee of three to study and report on the form of organization which would be best suited to the company in the new situation ahead. The members of the subcommittee were Harry Haskell, Chairman; Frederick Pickard and myself.

We spent several months studying the problem, consulting with industrialists in other companies, and conferring among ourselves. My own views were undoubtedly a reflection of Mr. Barksdale's management concepts. So were those of Haskell, who had served many years as Mr. Barksdale's right-hand man in the High Explosives Department. Pickard came around to sharing our judgment that a decentralized form of organization was most suitable, with both authority and accompanying responsibility delegated down the line.

We were just about ready to submit our report when Irenee brought to the Board a plan calling for a complete revamping of the Executive Committee, its nature to be mainly one of functional representation. This was adopted in April, 1919. Pickard and I, both former members, were retained on the Committee. At the same time, Irenee was made President of the Company, and Lammot duPont was named Chairman of the new Executive Committee.

I continued to serve on the Committee until transferred to General Motors some year and a half later, but along with Haskell and Pickard was greatly disappointed that the Haskell Committee had no chance of presenting its strong convictions regarding the desirable form of top organization. However, this incident did not diminish in the slightest degree the deep admiration and respect which I held for Irenee duPont.

While on this subject of decentralization, I might add that later on, at General Motors, I came across a report which Alfred P. Sloan had submitted in 1920 to Durant, then President. It urged reorganization of GM on the same basic principles which had been recognized by our group in the duPont Company. Durant had put it aside, much to Sloan's disappointment. In fact, he became so discouraged that he seriously considered leaving GM to accept a partnership in an outstanding firm of investment bankers. If Durant's retirement had not come about as it did, GM probably would have been deprived of the great benefits of Sloan's leadership over the ensuing years.

The fact that Sloan and I thought so squarely alike on principles of sound industrial organization unquestionably was one of the reasons why we worked so closely together during the formative years when the concept of decentralization was planted in the minds of all concerned.

In the post-war period I am speaking of, the automobile industry didn't rate very high with the banking fraternity, nor in the minds of the investing public. It was at that time Raskob made contributions to GM which proved to be decisive factors in the stability and growth of the corporation. As noted earlier, he and Pierre duPont were largely responsible for returning GM to the normal corporate status following the voting trust agreement, and of re-establishing Durant in the presidency. They reached an agreement whereby Durant would be responsible for operations, with duPont accepting responsibility for the financial affairs of the business.

Through Raskob's vision, the General Motors Acceptance Corporation was created, the first in the field of supplying credit to accommodate expanding consumer demand for automotive products. This was a tremendous accomplishment in the development of the automotive business.

In 1919 or 1920 added capital was required because of GM progress, and Raskob succeeded in selling a substantial block of common stock, with absorption by British interests and by a Canadian company owned largely by duPont Company and the same British interests. In conjunction with this, assistance was obtained by Raskob from important banking interests in New York, an accompanying accomplishment of which was the addition to the GM Board of outstanding representation from industry and banking. Among those added were Owen D. Young, Clarence Wooley and William Wooden, industrialists, and three banking representatives: E. R. Stettinius, Seward Prosser and George F. Baker, Jr. The latter three also assumed membership on the GM Finance Committee.

This stroke of genius on Raskob's part was the definite turning point for the automotive industry, in general, and for GM in particular. It gave the struggling new industry important standing and prestige, not only with banking interests but also with other investors and the general public. The new directors contributed markedly to the formulation of sound policies affecting the course of the business. And, what was crucial, it enabled General Motors to weather a storm which struck near the end of 1920. Without these top-flight individuals displaying their faith in the automotive business, it is doubtful whether GM would have survived.

The storm, when it broke, found the corporation with bank loans outstanding of more than $80 million. These debts had been contracted to meet the heavy expenditures incident to plant expansion and excessive inventories. The national economy had been suffering heavy strains, due chiefly to excesses of the early post-war period, and the stock market was in a perilous position.

Then one day in November of that year, to the consternation of Pierre duPont and Raskob, it was found that Durant was head over heels in debt through brokerage accounts. He had accumulated large holdings of GM common stock, purchased on margin, and there was great reason to fear that if his stock were forced into liquidation there would be repercussions leading to a general collapse in the stock market, with GM almost inevitably thrown into receivership.

Pierre duPont and Raskob struggled through the problem for long hours extending through an entire night, aided by the bankers represented on the Board. Then early one memorable morning, I and other members of the duPont Finance Committee had a call for an immediate and emergency meeting in New York. We went up from Wilmington.

By the time the Committee convened, there had been worked out a plan whereby all of Durant's GM holdings would be taken over by a subsidiary company, the duPont Securities Company, to be used solely for this purpose. The duPont Company undertook to transfer to the treasury of this subsidiary company a substantial block of GM stock owned by itself, and in addition the bankers had arranged for a one-year loan of $20 million. The day was saved.

The plan gave Durant a 40 per cent interest in the common, or equity, stock of duPont Securities Company, but he was required, under insistence from the banking interests, to retire completely from the General Motors management. Shortly thereafter, the duPont Company, responding to his overtures, purchased his stock in the holding company. Durant used the proceeds to finance a new venture in the automotive business, the Durant Motors Company.

The story of this episode in November, 1920, would not be complete without mention of something which occurred during the year before. A one-week trip in a private railroad car was arranged to permit members of the duPont Finance Committee to visit GM plant operations in Detroit and other places around the country. I was in the group. On numerous occasions during that trip, one of the men pointed out the economic storm warnings which were gathering on the horizon. Repeatedly he uttered gloomy prophecies, warning of a decline in the stock market. In the light of events which took place late the following year, it is indeed ironic that this man, whose conspicuous pessimism was not shared by others on the journey, was W. C. Durant!

The duPont Company, in bailing out Durant, resorted to emergency bank borrowings, as noted above, to the extent of $20 million in one-year obligations. Before the end of 1921, the one-year notes were refunded, and additional capital was raised through the issuance of ten-year notes in the amount of $35 million. This additional enforced investment in GM was regarded by the duPont Company as a temporary measure, and ways and means were sought whereby within the 10-year period the Company could liquidate its excess holdings of GM stock.

Upon urging by Pierre duPont and Raskob, I gave extended thought to the matter, and early in 1923 conveyed to them a suggestion which they accepted and which led, after months of joint consideration by duPont and GM authorities, to the creation of the Managers Securities Company. The company was formed with $5 million of common stock of two classes, and $28 million of preferred stock. GM subscribed to the common stock, duPont Company subscribing to the preferred.

General Motors then held the common stock available for sale at cost to a selected group of its executives who were adjudged deserving on the basis of the potential value of their services. Within the year 1923, approximately 80 such individuals active in the GM organization had been selected by a special committee composed of Board members not eligible to participate. Offerings of the stock were made to these employees, to the extent of the major part of the common stock outstanding, a small portion being reserved for later offering as top-flight personnel subsequently proved ability to contribute to progress of the business.

The plan also provided for the liquidation by the duPont Company of its preferred stock in Managers Securities Company during the eight years remaining of the 10-year notes. This was achieved through a contract with GM which represented a striking example of the strong faith held by the duPont Company management in the values of the owner-management principle.

General Motors at that time had a bonus plan in effect, established in 1918, which provided annual awards to operating personnel who were contributing most to constructive service of the company's interests. The amount available for such awards was determined as a stipulated percentage of net earnings over and above a given return on invested capital. The contract with Managers Securities Company provided that beginning in 1923, one half of the amounts available for bonus awards would be paid by GM annually for eight years to Managers Securities Company. The proceeds, under this contract, would be used to retire preferred stock of the company held by the duPont Company, after deduction for payment of preferred stock dividends and administrative costs.

It was anticipated that this arrangement would result in complete retirement of the preferred stock within eight years. But because of the successful accomplishments of GM management, proceeds from the bonus award fund were larger than anticipated, with the result that the preferred stock was retired in something like six years. During the remaining period of the contract, Managers Securities Company invested the surplus payments received in additional shares of GM stock.

It is the solid conviction of everyone familiar with the great progress and accomplishments of GM during those years that they derived to a large degree from the incentives created by the Managers Securities Company plan, coupled with the concepts of coordinated, decentralized management control which were firmly implanted in the same period. Executives throughout the far-flung operating divisions of the Corporation, through their equity holdings of Company stock, came to recognize that their own welfare was tied up with the welfare of all GM stockholders.

Raskob regarded the plan as "his baby," and rightfully so, since he was the driving force which led to its application. Once in the late 20's, Raskob in a public utterance said the Managers Security Company "had made 80 millionaires." The remark, which received much attention and is still occasionally quoted, referred to the 80 chosen employees who were original subscribers to the Managers Security Company stock.

What about the position of duPont Company stockholders, who voluntarily surrendered that GM stock in order to make it available to GM executives? It is my firm conviction, and one widely shared, that the residual stock remaining in the hands of the duPont Company today is worth far more than would be the value of its GM investment if the company had held on to that stock 34 years ago.

As for myself, well, I was among the 80 employees referred to by Raskob. To pay for Managers Security Company stock, I sold duPont stock which I owned. With sufficient collateral available, what a pity I didn't borrow the money from a bank!

Meanwhile, back in 1920, with the departure of Durant from the scene, General Motors was faced with the necessity of a major reorganization among top management. The bankers were insistent that no one except Pierre duPont could provide the leadership required. He had retired from active business life, and was loathe to take on heavy responsibilities of the new assignment. After much persuasion, however, he was prevailed upon to accept the presidency, but with the understanding that his tenure would end as soon as a suitable successor could be found. In 1923 that successor was found in the person of Alfred P. Sloan, Jr., who had been operating vice president. He continued to serve the company magnificently for many years afterwards.

Pierre duPont recognized the need for a radical reorganization of GM under his leadership. Raskob, as Chairman of GM's Finance Committee, was working closely with him in carrying it out. Thus was the stage set for the next milestone, and a crucial one, in my own business career.

CHAPTER IV

New Challenges at General Motors

One day early in December of 1920 I was confronted with one of the hardest decisions of my life. John Raskob, as Chairman of GM's Finance Committee, invited me to separate myself from executive duties with the duPont Company and assume the position of Vice President in Charge of Finance in General Motors Corporation, with membership on the Board and on the Finance Committee.

Within a week or so, I decided to accept; the change became effective on January 1, 1921. Naturally, this led to my resignation as Treasurer and member of the duPont Executive Committee. However, I retained, and still do, my membership on the Finance Committee of that company.

In taking up my new duties with GM, it was clear that there was need for radical steps to bring about better coordinated control over the corporation's growing operations. Here was a stimulating challenge, and I launched at once into activities having that general objective. The busy and constructive years which followed found me, along with others, pioneering in the development of principles and techniques which would produce more effective management of the financial phases of the business.

In the corporation, expanding rapidly, there were complex issues to a large extent uncharted by business precedent. Naturally, their solution came about by evolutionary processes, progressively over the years. What made them especially complex was the need always to consider each policy in relation to principles of decentralization; it was vital that GM should not be deprived of the advantages inherent in permitting management at all levels to exercise the initiative, resourcefulness and special know-how which can be applied most effectively from experience on the "firing line."

Prior to 1921, inventories had gotten completely out of hand throughout the divisions, and were in a highly unbalanced state. The operating divisions had been proceeding more or less autonomously, with no control exercised from the central office over material commitments and purchase. In the latter part of 1920, with the corporation borrowing heavily from the banks, to considerable degree because of excessive inventory investment, the Finance Committee appointed a central Inventory Committee, headed by John L. Pratt, to gain control over the situation.

After my entry in GM at the start of 1921, I naturally came into contact with Mr. Pratt in connection with the inventory control problems, and we agreed that the emergency committee plan which had been established could not satisfactorily meet the corporation's requirements over the long pull. No such committee could possibly have sufficient familiarity with the detailed considerations involved in the orderly purchase and procurement of materials for all divisions. Instead, each division had to be counted on to gauge its own commitments in the light of reasonable expectancy of movement of finished products into the hands of consumers.

At the same time, it was recognized that effective central office control was necessary to insure orderly purchase of materials and to safeguard against the bad inventory situation which had prompted the establishment of the central Inventory Committee late in 1920.

Discussions led to a plan, carrying Mr. Pratt's full approval, which was submitted by me to the Finance Committee under date of April 21, 1921, and which was approved unanimously by the Finance Committee and became the basis of central office control. The report set down the fundamental principle that "the operating units themselves must of necessity be looked to as the primary seat of control of inventories." The interposition of an inventories committee, with its delegated powers, "affords a condition of dual responsibility which in normal conditions is unwholesome and objectionable."

Two chief aspects of inventory control were pointed out: First, the necessity of holding stocks on hand and en route to a minimum point calculated to afford measurable assurance against shut-down for lack of materials; and second, the hazard of basing commitments on inaccurate forecasts, and of losses from price changes or obsolescence. Among major considerations bearing on such commitments are the degree of confidence that may reasonably be placed in requirement estimates; the probable price trends; the condition of suppliers, and the form and conditions of contract commitments.

"All (of these) are essentially operating problems," the memorandum stated, "and can be best dealt with by the operating organization. Insofar as the whole involves the matter of working capital requirements, the Finance Committee must have its voice reflected in the control, but this had better be by way of rules covering points of general policy rather than by any attempt at direct action. Moreover, it would seem logical and sound in organization principle for the Vice President or Chief Executive in charge of operations to be looked to to see that the divisions effectively control inventories in accord with Finance Committee policies or good business practice."

The plan required the divisions to submit monthly forecasts of production schedules four months ahead, and it prescribed limitations on commitments and procurement of materials to the approved schedule. Such planning by the divisions required forecasts of sales, to which production schedules necessarily must be tied. Opportunities were provided for central office scrutiny of sales forecasts, and to consider whether they appeared realistic. Procurement of materials for needs beyond requirements of the four-month forecasts was classified as "forward commitments," and required advance submittal to the governing committee of the Board for approval.

Principles adopted in that 1921 report, and the inventory control methods it established, including the monthly forecasting, have remained in effect in General Motors to the present day. Among my duties when in charge of finance was the scrutinizing of monthly forecasts, and the raising of questions when estimates of future sales appeared out of line with basic trends and conditions. It fell my lot, over the years, to maintain almost constant contact with the several divisions on these matters; discussions were held, and attempts made to rationalize forecasts of retail sales. Frequently, these discussions led to revisions of forecasts, and to corresponding adjustments of production schedules, but always the final determination was left to each division. The central office did not presume to impose revisions of forecasts.

Much was done also, step-by-step, to improve techniques of forecasting in the financial department itself, thus equipping the department to deal more realistically with the planning of capital expenditures and the control of inventories. The economist who had been serving in a consulting capacity in the duPont Company accepted transfer to General Motors, as did several analysts who had been in the duPont financial department.

Within a year or so after my entry into GM, and after surveying the considerable talent available within the corporation, I secured the transfer of Albert Bradley as principal assistant on my staff in New York. He proved a tower of strength as we moved forward in developing more effective, coordinated financial control. Mr. Bradley reached the age of retirement in the middle of 1956, and is now Chairman of the Board of General Motors.

In conjunction with the monthly forecasting procedure, which afforded the basis of inventory controls, we introduced also a form by which each division was required to submit monthly reports on the financial results of its operations. A specimen of such form is reproduced on page 129, in the Appendix.

This form was designed with a view not only of eliciting the data desired but also of planting in the minds of the reporting divisions the significance of the various factors involved. As can be seen from the form, each factor has a bearing on the return on investment, which is the end result sought. The investment items (bottom of form) are shown in terms of ratio to sales, with the reciprocal of the sum total representing the rate of turnover of investment. At the same time, the costs and expense items in the various categories are shown as a percentage of sales. The difference between the sum total of these and 100 per cent represents the percentage of net profit on sales. The previous chapter gave some description of the genesis and applicability of the mathematical formula $R = T \times P$, where there is represented return on investment, rate of turnover of investment and profit as a percentage of sales. In calling upon the divisions to report the financial results of their operations within the framework of this formula, the underlying thought was to bring about a greater consciousness of the significance of the factors involved, and an appreciation as to how improvement in overall results could be achieved by suitable attention to each element of investment, cost or expense. This method of reporting contributed importantly to a better understanding of the end results sought, and to the furtherance of efforts toward effective coordinated control.

Principles to guide the pricing of products in the corporation also were adopted in the early 20's. They were discussed comprehensively in a series of articles published in 1924 in "Management and Administration," under the title, "Pricing Policy in Relation to Financial Control." The first article outlined the principles involved; the second explained the methods of analysis used, and the third gave illustrations of the pricing policies in application. Reviewing these articles now, I find them to be an adequate account of the matter. Consequently, I have included them in the Appendix. Since it will not be necessary here to deal with the subject at any length, I will limit myself to a few general comments.

The pricing policy adopted more than three decades ago still remains in effect in GM commercial operations, and has demonstrated its practical adaptability over the years on many critical occasions. A particular difficulty in the automotive business is the seasonal fluctuation in sales volumes, and the virtual impossibility of operating plants at a uniform rate through the year. The same difficulty arises during longer periods of depressed sales volume, when there appears to be a strong incentive to raise prices in an attempt to maintain a normal rate of return on investment.

A fundamental concept of the GM pricing policy is the establishment of a "standard volume," which represents a given plant's ability to produce over the years, assuming plant capacity is balanced and in line with reasonable expectancy of demand. The "standard volume" also takes cyclical fluctuations into account.

In the application of this criterion, the tendency is avoided to increase prices in periods of subnormal volume and to lower them in boom periods. The resultant pricing of products tends to lessen the deepening of troughs and the raising of peaks in the course of the business cycle.

Costs and expenses are measured similarly by a "standard volume." Where plant capacity exceeds what is considered necessary to meet a realistic expectancy of volume, the "standard volume" application automatically eliminates the fixed investment relating thereto, as though the excess capacity did not exist.

The attainable return on investment is, of course, subject to competitive influence. The pricing policy of GM is to seek that rate of return, on the basis of "standard volume," which experience indicates is attainable from an economic standpoint. This has led to the determination of rate which has stood up over the years, and which has been proven attainable under the intense competitive conditions existing.

The policy mentioned was designed to apply only in the case of finished automotive products, i.e., cars and trucks. The situation with regard to component parts and accessories is somewhat different. The vehicle manufacturing divisions are dependent upon a vast array of suppliers for parts and accessories, many of them outside companies, some of them small, wholly-owned divisions of

GM itself. These subsidiary divisions are themselves representative of "small business," operating in the climate of free enterprise. During the years of John L. Pratt's activities, all were under his direct jurisdiction, under policies of decentralized responsibilities. A spirit of competition was engendered, too; the divisions were expected to meet the prices available from outside independent suppliers, to the extent that the facts bearing on this matter could be reliably ascertained.

During the extended period of depression following the 1929 crash, this pricing principle was rigidly adhered to, in spite of markedly subnormal profits. It is believed that had there been an attempt, during the low levels of 1931, to raise prices above the defined "standard price," in order to improve return on investment, the effect inevitably would have been a further depression in consumer demand.

In the years when Herbert Hoover was Secretary of Commerce, I had some opportunities of discussing with him General Motors' policies in forecasting and planning, and the underlying theories of our pricing policies. He recognized that the automotive industry occupied a unique position in that only its dealers stood between the manufacturer and the ultimate consumer; it had no other intermediate distribution channels. There was no unavoidably hidden inventory of products, as in the case of the steel industry and other segments of the economy where there existed multiple intermediates, such as fabricators and merchandise suppliers. Consequently, it was possible for the automotive industry to gain a direct and accurate measure of the finished product inventory in relation to retail movement.

As Secretary of Commerce, Mr. Hoover had been striving to set in motion machinery which would accumulate and maintain reliable statistics on the national inventory situation. His object was to gain from reports of industrial establishments, assembled by the Department of Commerce, facts as to inventories throughout numerous segments of industry. These facts would be disseminated among primary manufacturers, serving to advise them of the situation, thus minimizing the disruptions to basic production and employment which occurs when these facts are belatedly discovered. The Secretary was much interested in learning of the methods GM employed toward the same end. He recognized, however, the difficulties experienced by other manufacturers dependent upon flow of products through multiple intermediaries. Corresponding data are not available to them.

Even in General Motors, where only direct contact with its dealers was necessary to obtain inventory data, the collection and analysis of accurate information were not easy to achieve. Efforts were made during the early 20's to persuade the several car and truck divisions to obtain regular reports from their dealers, showing the movements of new and used vehicles and the stock of unsold vehicles on hand. But the idea wasn't "sold" until 1924, and then by reason of a very unusual and somewhat dramatic incident.

In the course of several months, we in the central office became convinced, from analysis of registration statistics supplied by R. L. Polk & Co., that the automobile divisions were over-producing, and especially the Chevrolet Division. But in a meeting with Mr. Sloan, at which I was present, the General Sales Manager of that Division insisted we were wrong. He was "sure" there was not over-production, and said that he knew more about the situation in the field than any of us could who were remote from it.

Then in the spring of 1924 Mr. Sloan went out on what was to become a periodic field trip to call on dealers. The first stop on this particular journey was St. Louis, where a day was spent. I went along, and subsequently accompanied him on all such field trips. In the course of calling on GM dealers in St. Louis, it became obvious that they had excessive inventories of new cars. The next stop at Kansas City revealed a similar situation.

On the train out of Kansas City we drafted a telegram,

which Mr. Sloan sent to General Manager William Knudsen, of the Chevrolet Division, instructing him to cut the production schedule, and laying down a definite schedule for the next three months.

The situation was serious, and this drastic step doubtless was called for. But it is the only instance I can recall, in all the years, when Mr. Sloan undertook to dictate a course of action on the part of a division manager. Indeed, this single exception to the rule points up sharply the fact that GM management was characterized by an absence of such dictation from the top.

Prior to that particular period, I had been called on by Mr. Sloan to assume chairmanship of a group concerning itself with the broad problems of policy involved in the distribution and sales of automotive products. The St. Louis and Kansas City dealer inventory incident, and Mr. Sloan's telegram, naturally led to full discussion of this problem in the group, which urged the divisions to require regular reports from their dealers. As a result a plan was inaugurated for 10-day reports, a practice still continuing today, and adopted industry-wide in recent years.

It will be observed that the sales and distribution group did not "order" adoption of the intended procedure; it possessed no administrative authority to do so. What it did was to present available facts, and bring to the attention of the operating divisions the procedures and principles which seemed best capable of improving dealer relations and the general economics of distribution and sales. Its function might be described as "factual persuasions."

There had been a marked tendency within GM divisions, as well as throughout the industry, to over-pack dealerships in areas of high potential, with the result that in many such areas opportunities for profitable operations by individual dealers were seriously jeopardized. This matter was given earnest consideration by our central policy group, which recognized that if the dealer body could not operate profitably — the mortality rate had

GM EXECUTIVES AND DIRECTORS, GUESTS May 15, 1923 AT DINNER OF THE MUNCIE (IND.) CHAMBER OF COMMERCE. L. to R.: Top row: Charles F. Kettring, Donaldson Brown, Henry F. Crane, John L. Pratt, Charles S. Mott and E. F. Johnson. Bottom row: George Whitney, Junius S. Morgan, Jr., Alfred P. Sloan, Jr., C. E. Wilson, W. S. Knudsen, Walter S. Carpenter and R. Samuel McLaughlin.

become alarming — the time would come when the Corporation itself would have to take on the retailing of its products.

Such a course was unthinkable. First of all, the capital requirement would be of unmanageable proportions. But even more serious would be the loss of an organization of independent dealers, each functioning competitively with the incentive of his own enlightened self-interest. There is no adequate substitute for this incentive in business operations.

The result of these considerations led to a central staff study of suitable forms to meet the dealer needs in financial accounting. Another objective was to bring about uniformity in accounting practices among dealers, so that we would in the future be able to keep apprised of the facts. After the forms were put into use, we did procure regularly from a large segment of GM dealers the reports on their financial operations.

It was later that the inauguration of 10-day dealer reports of stocks of new and used cars, and movements at retail occurred. These data enabled our central staff to scrutinize divisional forecasts of sales on a much more realistic basis. Seasonal characteristics were appraised from historical analysis of monthly registration figures. Reflections as to the profit position of the dealers were taken into account, with attempts to identify situations where there might be undue influences occasioned by over-supply, leading to forced movement of vehicles at retail, with consequent loss to the dealers.

My duties included continual analysis of the 10-day reports. When individual forecasts and associated production schedules seemed to be out of line with basic trends, I would contact the operating division concerned, as referred to previously. The relationship was a wholesome one, and the continued functioning along this line eventually contributed a great deal toward better coordinated control of financial affairs throughout the corporation.

These were evolutionary developments; during the years

I served as Chairman of the Sales and Distribution Policy Group, we made considerable progress in arriving at fundamental decisions which laid the ground work for later development of specific operational procedures. However, in time, R. H. Grant was transferred from General Sales Manager of Chevrolet to the central staff, and replaced me as Group Chairman, and it was then that these theories came to be better crystalized, and progressively put into procedural acceptance. I remained as a member of this particular central office group, and over subsequent years contributed as I was able to the gradual implementation of policies and principles for which the foundation previously had been laid during my temporary regime.

During the 20's, it was found that in certain spots throughout the country there were potential opportunities for retailing GM products but that the several divisions had not been able to attract to these open points individual dealers willing to risk the necessary capital. As stated earlier, we had decided it was important to preserve the basic structure of independent dealers, functioning as individual entrepreneurs. We believed it was important to avoid entry by GM into the direct field of retailing. Also we recognized that "small business" has a vital function to perform in the nation's economy.

To overcome the difficulty of finding dealers for the so-called open points, there was created in 1929 what was then known as Motors Holding Company, a 100 per cent owned subsidiary. (In 1936, for technical legal reasons, the company was dissolved and the activity taken over as a GM division.) Since World War II, the activity has been expanded materially. It continues to play an important role in the retailing of GM products, and important competitors in recent years have imitated GM's example.

Motors Holding was set up to identify, in collaboration with each of the operating divisions, the so-called "open locations" where a division had been unable to find competent dealers able to invest the capital required. In such cases, franchises were given to competent dealers having only limited capital available, with Motors Holding providing the major portion of needed funds. A profit-sharing plan was worked out whereby a share of the profits earned by the dealer would be applied to the indebtedness, with emphasis on paying it off as rapidly as possible, so that the dealer could gain the status of an independent merchant.

Motors Holding seeks no special favors of any kind for its dealers; they operate under the same contract and under the same conditions as all GM dealers. Motors Holding leaves the management entirely to its dealers, but endeavors in every case to establish sound financial policies which result in greater sales and profits. Incidentally, this intimate contact by the corporation with problems of dealer management also contributed to the evolutionary formation of basic distribution policies by GM. Motors Holding dealers serve as a sort of proving ground.

In 1949, a great many dealers who had been established in business through financing by Motors Holding had paid off their obligations. A large group of them gave a testimonial dinner that year to Mr. Sloan and to me. (I was thus honored because the Motors Holding activity had been under my direct jurisdiction.) In an address that evening, reviewing the 20 years of successful activities of Motors Holding, I took occasion to point out how this method of distribution was in accordance with the fundamental decentralization policy of General Motors.

"One of the most fundamental policies of the corporation," I said, "is to assure the preservation of a sound, virile and profitable retailing organization, comprising dealers who are independent merchants, and who are inspired in the exercise of individual initiative through the driving force of owner-management."

In the same address, I digressed briefly from the affairs of Motors Holding to touch upon an economic-political issue which continues to confuse and bemuse us.

"I am sure all of us have been perplexed and grieved over the trends we have witnessed in this country toward what I might sum up as 'stateism' . . . . . . Pressure group forces of all kinds, some conflicting, play upon those in political office. Great confusion has existed whereby the American public has been brought to seriously distorted notions concerned with what is truly in the interests of social security. We have the innumerable 'do-gooders' who are pressing for a planned economy, or the nationalization of industry, a la Great Britain. I quote from an interview with one of this turn of mind. He said:

> '— if it were possible to intelligently administer and guide the affairs of so large and complex an institution as General Motors, affecting as it does the lives and welfare of so many people, influenced as it is by so many conditions over which it has no control, then I don't see why that same management ability and control could not be applied to the affairs of a nation with equally desirable results.'

"I don't know whether you think as highly of General Motors management as does the person whom I have just quoted. However, I want to put this to you:

"How do you think you would fare if those determining production and distribution policies were established in their positions of power through popular election or political appointment? Their term of office would be tenuous and transitory. Their alleged grasp of social considerations would be displayed by the handing down of directives to division managers — army fashion. In turn, these directives would have to be passed on down the line and observance required on the part of zone managers and the field men with whom you come into contact.

"These men now usually realize you know more about your immediate problems than they do. It is not intended that they try to tell you how to run your business. Their purpose is quite different; they are in close touch with your problems, and in this way supply a vital link in the chain of coordinated planning and control. It will be different if we should come into a new order of things such as I have envisioned. Would you like that new order of things?

"I leave the answer to you."

CHAPTER V

Basic Policies of Corporate Management

Large industrial organizations such as General Motors Corporation possess obvious economic advantages. Greater economy in purchasing is possible, for example, when larger quantities of materials are purchased. Every division in the company benefits from the new processes and techniques developed through the research, engineering and production experience of all other divisions. The public prestige of a large and well-known manufacturer likewise is an important asset to its advertising and distribution programs. Energetic and successful dealers are attracted to its banners. The company's institutional values also strengthen it from the standpoint of the investing public.

But large industrial combinations have disadvantages, too, the most serious of which is the problem of securing efficient management. This could be particularly true of a company like General Motors which engages in the manufacture and distribution of a wide variety of products. Obviously, it is humanly impossible for the GM Board of Directors or its Executive Committee or any group in top management to maintain the same kind of intimate contact with the details of its business as would be practicable in a smaller organization, or even in a large one engaged in less diversified business.

But the responsibility of a Board to the stockholder-owners of a business is exactly the same whether the business is small or large. That responsibility is to see to it that the business is operated in the true and long-range interest of the owners. Therefore, the proper organization of control is forced by absolute necessity. In GM we called this organization "decentralized operations and responsibilities, with coordinated control." It consists of a structure and management principles under which company policies, determined on the basis of full knowledge of all aspects of the business, can be effectively disseminated throughout the entire organization, and acted upon; at the same time preserving at all levels of management maximum freedom for the exercise of judgment and initiative in administrative decisions.

This kind of coordinated control is vital. Without it, the business would be better split up into various units, with separate ownership, even if this meant sacrificing the advantages inherent in the GM structure as it is.

I was privileged during the years of my activity in GM to play a part in the evolution of the fundamental management principles which made possible the attainment of this coordinated control. On assuming the position of Vice President in Charge of Finance, in January of 1921, I had had no previous contact with the automotive industry. I knew that I would be looked upon as an interloper by some in the organization who were experienced in dealing with problems relating to engineering, production, purchasing, and sales.

Nevertheless, I had administrative jurisdiction over financial phases of the business, and from the standpoint of the Board of Directors, representing the owners of the business, these financial matters obviously were of prime significance to the sound management of the company. The general test of efficiency of management of any business is the rate of return on capital employed. Capital is entitled to a varying rate of return, largely dependent upon competitive conditions in the broad sense, and in the hazard that is involved. Needless to say, good will — that intangible and illusive but none-the-less valuable asset which every business seeks to enjoy — is of great importance.

Apart from this, however, profit from industry is dependent upon the character of product and the skill in processes and in methods of manufacture, advertising and distribution. At the same time, the rate of return on capital is affected directly by the control of the investment in working capital items and fixed assets, in relation to the volume of the business. Capital employed in the production and sale of a product that is bought on the basis of exact specifications, and in which no highly specialized knowledge is required for manufacture and distribution, contents itself with a relatively low rate of return. The production of an article that is exclusive in design, possessing superior engineering qualities and carrying with it a peculiar appeal to fashion or the taste of the public affords to capital the opportunity of enjoying a commensurate rate of return. The hazard which accompanies such an enterprise is minimized by the exercise of skill in progressive engineering improvements, and in ingenuity in anticipating the changing tastes of the buying public.

In gauging the effectiveness of management the first approach always is to examine the over-all result, which is the rate of return on capital employed. If this be subnormal, having due regard to the character of business and the competitive situation, it is self-evident that something is wrong with the management. The second step is to identify the cause — and correct it. Thus in a very real sense, the financial phases with which I was concerned at GM were fundamental to the prosperity and sound growth of the business.

It seemed to me that my task, in those early years, was to find some means whereby the significant accounting facts and financial considerations affecting the business would be revealed. Then it would be necessary to get them understood and appreciated by those who were responsible for the various operations; management at all levels must be made more aware of the constructive opportunities which existed for serving better the long-term interests of the stockholders.

With my associates on the financial staff, I recognized that we could not secure effective control of financial policies by arbitrary edict. You can't cram basic policy down the throats of those who must be depended upon to carry them out and expect good results. Everyone concerned in the organization must be brought to understand and to accept, in spirit, the validity of the policies imposed.

Moreover, sound policies cannot be formulated without the cooperation and assistance of personnel all the way up and down the line. There must be, in fact, a "two-way flow" in managerial human relations. The downward flow begins with authority at the top level of management, and continues down through all echelons of management, each responsible within the limits of assigned jurisdiction for administering established company policy. The upward flow consists of questions, facts and opinions arising out of actual experience in all phases of the business. These are vital to the sound determination of policy, and must be allowed to exert proper pressure in policy formulation.

This kind of two-way flow is essential for the simple reason that in a big, complex industrial combination it is impossible for top management to lay down policy in terms sufficiently explicit to eliminate the need for the broad exercise of judgment by employees who must execute policy. In a small enterprise, where one man can keep his finger on every detail of the business, the situation is quite different. Large industrial units can achieve the same end result only by the kind of broad coordinated policy control which I am describing.

There is another reason why this two-way flow of ideas and information is indispensable to modern business. Everything in the field of industrial management depends upon and revolves around human impulses and human relations. Participation in the formulation of policy, and in its execution, plays an important part in developing the self-reliance and potentialities of the individual.

Even if it were possible, in the name of efficiency, to eliminate the need for individual initiative through cut-and-dried directives from an infallible superior, that would be a wrong course to follow. The effect upon the character and the spirit of the human beings involved would be tragic. In our human frailty, we need encouragement, an occasional pat on the back, the solid satisfaction of individual accomplishment and proper recognition of a job well done.

If all those on whom we depend for the production of goods and services were to become mere automatons, then the priceless ingredients of our free society — self-reliance, pride of workmanship, and individual initiative — would be destroyed. Compulsion would take the place of leadership. Political intrigue would replace efficiency. Expediency would usurp the throne of sound judgment. We are all mortal beings, with the faults and weaknesses of human nature, but if our society is to survive we must hold unalterably to faith in the dignity and worth of the individual. Surely this must be of paramount concern in the formulation of policies truly serving the long-range interests of the owners of any business dependent upon that society.

Such were the considerations which influenced us in those early years. As mentioned earlier, Mr. Sloan always was heartily in accord with our thinking in this respect; perhaps it would be more fitting for me to say that he and I worked companionately when concerned in those areas. It would be hard to say which of us supplied the initiative in the course of numerous activities designed to achieve effective coordinated control in the affairs of General Motors.

As indicated, this matter of "control" is the crux of good industrial management. All of us appreciate the importance of promoting initiative and enthusiastic effort down the line by delegating authority and responsibility. The difficulty in executive management is not failing to recognize the advantage of decentralization; rather, it is in knowing where limitations should be placed, in order to gain the necessary coordination with a minimum of interference with administrative decisions.

The answer is not found in any particular or precise line of demarcation; you cannot draw a line across an organization chart and say that it represents the limits of decentralization, or that those who are above the line shall be concerned with basic policy and those below it concerned only with purely administrative affairs. That's not how a successful enterprise operates.

The solution rather must come through the formulation of broad concepts which, once promulgated and understood throughout the corporation, could serve to bring about genuine and effective coordination. The first premise, which I have mentioned, is that everything possible must be done to encourage initiative, self-reliance and pride of achievement in the individual. A two-way flow of ideas and information is necessary, together with full exercise of judgment at every level of management in the execution of agreed-upon corporate policies in the spirit of their intent.

At the same time, it must be recognized that no institution or organized group can be free from authoritative direction, nor can its objectives be realized without obedience to properly constituted authority. The nature of authority, of course, varies between wide limits. In a dictatorship, authority is the arbitrary whim and fancy of a dictator. Authority in the United States is that body of law, established by constitutional processes, which implements an ideal and which imposes upon every public servant and every private citizen certain courses of action which are presumed to be in the public interest. It is obvious that freedom of action in the political sphere must be within the framework of law.

Similarly, in the field of industrial management, freedom of action must be within the framework of policy. The authority over any given industrial enterprise is that of policy which is based on a balanced consideration of the interests of the investor, the employee and the consumer. Such policy, once formulated, must exercise control over the actions of the entire personnel; everyone from the president down must conform to that policy.

It can be seen that the effectuation of these concepts in a large corporation depends first upon the proper management structure, and then, importantly, upon an effective and continuing educational process which succeeds in developing a thorough understanding and appreciation of the adopted policies and the reasons for them in relation to the fundamental objectives of the business.

The basic responsibility for control of the business rests, of course, with the Board of Directors, representing the stockholders. But this Board, or subcommittee acting for it, should not attempt to make purely executive decisions. That would be committee management. Committee action is by majority vote; executive action is by individual choice. Where committee action is applied to problems of purely administrative management, the result is almost always bad. As the saying goes, "what is everybody's business is nobody's business." The Board or Executive Committee, therefore, must fulfill its responsibility of centralized control without unduly interfering with the executive administration of the organization. This becomes the first problem in the establishment of a sound organization structure. It is met by careful definition of the duties and responsibilities of the Board of Directors or its Executive Committee. The following indicates the basis for such definition which was worked out in the 1920's in General Motors and which still applies in principle to any large corporation:

1. The Executive Committee (or Board) must have a thorough knowledge of the characteristics of the business and an understanding of how the lines of authority are drawn in the operations, and the extent to which activities in all departments are coordinated. For this purpose, the Committee requires frequent briefing by executive personnel, plus such statistical analyses and other information as may be necessary for a complete knowledge of the enterprise.

2. Wherever practicable, the Committee or Board should lay down a concrete policy, establishing the fundamental basis upon which the activity or any or all departments shall be predicated. This can be done only where it is possible to express a point of policy in clear terms, capable of inter-

pretation and proper application in the varied conditions which are likely to occur.

3. In the many cases where it is impossible to lay down any general rules, and yet where questions of policy are involved, the Committee must deal with problems as they arise. Since there is always danger of encroaching upon the sphere of administrative management, it is of great importance to analyze the characteristics of each problem so that it can be dealt with solely from the policy standpoint. Having given responsibility to the management personnel for the administrative conduct of the business, the Directors should never at any time withdraw the corresponding authority necessary for effective performance.

4. The President, as the chief executive officer, is the connecting link between policy and administrative control. He must distinguish clearly between them as problems arise; one of his important functions is to make sure there is no undue interference with the prerogatives of individuals in the organization. When there is room for doubt as to what may be best for the welfare of the stockholders, he must obtain from the Executive Committee or Board an expression of policy. In all other respects, it is his duty to see that executives all down the line have the latitude and authority warranted, with a full sense of responsibility for their assigned tasks.

5. In rare cases and under unusual circumstances, where it is not practicable to draw the distinction between policy and administration, it may be justified for the Executive Committee to assume the responsibility for direct action in administrative matters. But it should be avoided if possible; if done, care should be taken to point out to all affected personnel the factors which made such action necessary.

In the case of General Motors, the Board of Directors for many years delegated responsibilities and authority to two main governing committees. The Finance Committee, of which I became Chairman in 1928, succeeding Mr. Raskob, had control over accounting, in the broad sense; matters of dividend policy; expenditures exceeding designated amounts for specific projects aimed at development and progress of the business, and, of course, the determination of ways and means of financing capital expansion.

The Executive Committee, headed by Mr. Sloan, was assigned duties and responsibilities concerning operations. In the case of capital expenditures, the Executive Committee was called upon to appraise the validity of expenditures where projects called for administration on the part of operating divisions.

The specific duties and responsibilities of the two committees were clearly defined in corporation by-laws. However, as Mr. Sloan and I worked in close harmony over the years, we both recognized that while in theory the designated functions were separate and distinct, the fact was that in the management of a business as complex as GM there are, inescapably, areas in which the line between them cannot be clearly drawn. Over the years, on all matters of joint interest, I deferred to Mr. Sloan, who occupied the position of Chief Executive Officer. Together we labored to make effective that degree of coordinated control necessary for achievement of the objectives of both of the subcommittees functioning under the Board.

A great deal was accomplished in this direction through what were called central office "policy groups." These groups had no authorities but met to review and discuss current corporate problems. They assisted greatly in bringing about an understanding of policies among operating executives, and thus in securing more effective compliance with them. Also, the GM structure includes vice presidents serving in the capacity of "group executives," each embracing several operating divisions. These executives are not dictators; they are called on rather to keep in intimate contact with the operations in their respective jurisdictions, to serve in an advisory capacity, and to bring about common understanding of purposes and policies affecting divisional operations. In other words, the group executives are the top echelon liaison officers in the "two-way flow" of authority and ideas essential to proper coordinated control of corporation activities.

For many years, after revamping its Executive Committee in 1922, the basic organization structure of the duPont Company paralleled that of GM. The duPont Executive Committee has been composed of members without administrative authority (except the President of the Company himself). Each member serves in an advisory capacity, with a specifically assigned area of supervision, functioning much in the same way as those in group executive and staff executive positions in General Motors.

In 1937, however, after months of discussion, GM effected a radical reorganization of its management structure. The Finance and Executive Committees were abolished, replaced by a single governing committee designated as the Policy Committee. All duties and responsibilities previously held by the two governing groups were consolidated in the new nine-member Policy Committee.

The plan was conceived by Mr. Sloan. I subscribed to it wholeheartedly and enthusiastically. But Lammot duPont, then GM Chairman, and Walter S. Carpenter, Jr., a member of the Finance Committee, at first objected. Both were in top position in duPont, and both were wedded to the principle of separating the duties and responsibilities of the Board between finance and executive committees. Mr. Sloan and I had many sessions with the two men, separately and together, seeking to convince them of the merits of the reorganization. We argued that the conditions in GM were quite different from those in duPont; in the latter case, all authority was centered in Wilmington, whereas in GM broad matters of policy were centered in New York, with operations centered hundreds of miles away in Detroit. We felt that much benefit was gained by maintaining a comparatively objective treatment of policy considerations in New York, with the administrative management remaining in Detroit, and with policy groups and group executives helping to bring about the necessary coordinated treatment. Eventually, Mr. duPont and Mr. Carpenter agreed, and the reorganization was accomplished but it appeared then and later that both did so with "tongues in their cheeks."

About this time, I had serious ideas about retiring from active duties with GM. I had moved my family at the end of 1936 to Maryland, where I had taken on a dairy farm. But when I told Mr. Sloan what I had in mind, he opposed it vehemently, saying that if I would not carry on with him, he would abandon the reorganization plan. I, of course, was gratified by the warmth of his urging, and gave up my notion of retiring. However, I felt then, and did not find reason afterward to change my mind, that continuation of my personal activities was not essential. The principles of coordinated control were solidly planted, and from the standpoint of basic financial considerations, highly qualified men, led by Albert Bradley, were available to carry on in this sphere.

With the reorganization, by-laws were amended designating the Chairman of the Board as Chief Executive Officer, to which office Mr. Sloan was elected. At the same time, W. S. Knudsen was elected President. He stayed in Detroit, and the Chairman's headquarters remained in New York. I was elected Vice Chairman, also with headquarters continuing in New York. I had direct jurisdiction over the Finance Department, auxiliary financial activities, Motors Holding Division, and other specific duties as assigned by Mr. Sloan. I had no other administrative authority except, under the by-laws, the duties of the Chairman devolved on me in his absence. The reorganization became effective May 3, 1937, and the initial Policy Committee consisted of Mr. Sloan, as Chairman; Mr. Knudsen, C. E. Wilson, then Executive Vice President, Mr. Bradley, John Thomas Smith, and myself, as full-time employees, together with three Directors: Lammot duPont, Walter Carpenter and George Whitney. This structure remained in effect until the further reorganization in 1946.

Going back to 1928, no matter how wise and efficient may be the machinery for industrial management, problems can arise from unexpected and strange events. Such was the case in General Motors that year, when a situation arose which for a time seriously threatened to disrupt the harmonious relationships among the top flight personnel. It came about when Raskob, without consulting his GM associates, was elected to the chairmanship of the Democratic National Committee.

It appeared to Sloan and others that this action on the part of a man serving as Chairman of the Finance Committee would be construed by the public, and especially by political leaders throughout the country, as meaning that the Corporation was engaging in partisan politics. There was deep fear that the consequences would be damaging to the consumer good-will of the Corporation, and would have other adverse effects. Raskob, therefore, was urged to relinquish his political activity in the interest of General Motors.

Raskob was an ardent supporter of Al Smith, then an aspirant to the presidency, as also was Pierre duPont, both being motivated importantly by an earnest desire to bring about repeal of the prohibition law. Raskob held firmly to his view that his position with GM should not rule out his suitability as head of the Democratic party, and refused to withdraw. A distressing situation arose, the upshot of which was Raskob's resignation from the Board of Directors, as well as from chairmanship of the Finance Committee.

During the ensuing months, there was continuing hope on the part of all concerned that after the November election was over, Raskob would retire from his political activities and return to the Corporation which he had served with such distinction. The chairmanship of the Finance Committee was left open, with myself being designated as "Acting Chairman." At that time, I continued as Vice President in Charge of Finance.

It became settled around the middle of 1929 that Raskob would not return to General Motors. I was then elected Chairman of the Finance Committee, to succeed him, and Bradley succeeded me as Vice President in Charge of Finance.

This was the year when the country was approaching the stock market crash. Ahead was a period of receding economic activity, with deep depression to come in 1931 and 1932.

Dependable forecasting and planning were of outstanding importance during those difficult years. Production by all divisions was held in reasonable bounds, related to estimated forward demands for products, and inventories were held in reasonable balance. Car and truck prices were held in conformance with the corporation's basic pricing policy (Chapter IV).

The Corporation suffered marked depression in earnings, but was able to maintain dividend distributions at lower levels. General Motors experienced no demand on capital resources requiring at any point a resort to bank borrowing.

CHAPTER VI

Banks, Labor and Government

My election as Chairman of the Finance Committee of General Motors in 1929 marked a definite shift of emphasis in my business activities. During the period 1921 through the summer of 1929, I had been preoccupied largely by problems of internal management control in the corporation. Some of the fundamental principles evolved during that decade have been discussed in the previous chapters.

During the 1930's I found myself increasingly concerned with events transpiring outside of the corporation; events not directly related solely to GM operations, but with important impact upon its business affairs. As mentioned in the previous chapter, Albert Bradley succeeded me as Vice President in Charge of Finance, taking over my former duties. Free from the detailed responsibilities in connection with internal coordinated control, I gave more and more of my time to problems arising out of the interdependence of the corporation and the national welfare, and to broad questions of economic, social and political trends. I continued, of course, with primary concern over matters of coordinated financial control, and remained on most of the internal Policy Groups. Later I was designated by Sloan as his representative on matters related to labor policies.

There ensued years of depression, of radical political innovations, of marked stresses and strains in many relationships affecting business operations. From numerous memoranda, personal notes and published reports which I preserved from that period, I have selected four incidents on which to comment. One was the Detroit bank crisis early in 1932 which precipitated the Michigan bank holiday. Later, enactment of the National Industrial Recovery Act, with its celebrated Section 7 (a), set in motion a whole train of personnel problems in which I was deeply involved, not only in behalf of GM but also as Chairman of the automotive industry's NRA Industry Committee. In 1939 as Chairman of a Coordinating Committee of the National Association of Manufacturers, I interested myself actively in problems of joint interest to all industries, guiding the preparation of a "Declaration of Principles" which was adopted in 1939 by the Congress of American Industry. The fourth incident I have chosen from this period of a decade was the establishment within the GM organization of a committee to review the various developments in public affairs, and to interpret their probable impact upon the policies and program of the corporation. The committee was styled "Policy Group — Social and Economic Trends" and I was designated Chairman. In connection with this, I was also designated by Mr. Sloan as his representative concerned with government relations.

I fully appreciate the fact that it is difficult for any individual to be completely objective in appraising the significance of events in which he was personally involved. To some degree, my observations on these incidents will reflect personal impressions — perhaps even emotional reactions — which were experienced at the time. On the other hand, I now have the advantage of perspective, which is granted by the passage of years. Furthermore, in recounting these activities I have sought scrupulously to include only verifiable facts. One thing can be said with certainty: these incidents, and others which I have not touched upon, were part and parcel of a hectic and turbulent decade which reshaped much of the nation's political economy.

1. *Michigan Bank Holiday*

A whole generation has been born and grown up since the national bank crisis which attended the depression. But for the parents and grandparents of this new generation, it was an event never to be forgotten; one which directly affected every citizen and every institution in the land.

Signs of growing stress and strain on the banking structure first appeared in late 1932. Then in February, 1933, the first serious crisis arose in Detroit. I received word of it one Sunday morning, February 12, in a telephone call from Mr. Sloan, who told me that he and Walter Chrysler, President of the Chrysler Corporation, had been summoned to the White House and informed at breakfast with President Hoover the day before that the Reconstruction Finance Corporation had been asked to assist in a serious situation involving the Guardian Union Trust Company of Detroit. Secretary of the Treasury Ogden Mills, and a Mr. Miller representing R.F.C., attended the White House meeting.

Mr. Sloan said that he and Mr. Chrysler had been advised that R.F.C. considered it impracticable to extend the full amount of help that was deemed needed, and that it was hoped by the government that GM and Chrysler also would be willing to help out, thus permitting the bank to open on Tuesday morning, following the Lincoln Birthday holiday on Monday.

The President had laid great emphasis, Mr. Sloan told me, on the importance of dealing promptly with the situation, since a failure of the bank could have disastrous repercussions throughout the country. The Guardian Union Group in Detroit had a wide chain of affiliated banks in the State of Michigan. Mr. Chrysler was going out to Detroit that night, Mr. Sloan said, and he urged the importance of my going out also.

That telephone call touched off unremitting struggles which occupied a great deal of my time for many weeks. During a breathing spell a couple of weeks later, after returning home from Detroit, I dictated to my secretary a 19-page memorandum, virtually a personal diary, in which I recounted the whole story in detail while it was still fresh in my mind. The italicized quotations which follow are excerpted from that diary.

After talking with Mr. Sloan, I called up Mr. George Whitney, . . . as I felt there should be some banker in Detroit the following day on whom we could rely for advice and guidance. Mr. Whitney told me he thought Sloane Colt, President of the Bankers' Trust Company, was as intimately informed on affairs of the

Detroit Guardian Union Group as any New York banker. I called Mr. Colt . . . Later in the day he called back to say that he would take the Detroiter *out that night.*

Melville Traylor, the president of the First National Bank of Chicago, was in Sloane Colt's opinion the banker most familiar with the Detroit situation. He was summoned to Detroit also. I got on the train that evening at Harmon, found both Mr. Chrysler and Mr. Colt aboard, and we discussed the problem in a preliminary way. The next morning we were met at the station in Detroit by M. L. Prentis, GM Treasurer, and B. E. Hutchinson, of Chrysler. These two, together with Mr. Chrysler and myself, went immediately to a meeting in the Guardian National Bank.

At the meeting, presided over by Ernest T. Kanzler, the following were present: Messrs. Chrysler, Hutchinson, Alec Dow, of the Detroit Edison Company, Dr. Alfred Murphy, Chairman of the Board of the Guardian Group, and one or two others. Mr. Kanzler explained that R.F.C. and the administration in Washington at first had felt that something like $65 million was necessary to bolster up the situation, in view of the impending prospect of important runs on the institution, but later they had modified their views and appeared willing to render aid on the basis of $43 million being supplied by way of loans. The R.F.C. appeared willing to loan $37 million, to be secured by selected assets, and therefore there was required a minimum of $6 million to be loaned from other sources. At this stage, I think there was no intention of seeking assistance outside of Ford, General Motors, Chrysler and Detroit Edison Company.

Meanwhile, however, the situation had been complicated by two other developments. In Washington, Senator Couzens, of Michigan, made a strong statement in which he warned that if R.F.C. extended a loan to Guardian Union Trust Company, or any affiliate of the Guardian Detroit Union Group, which was not absolutely sound, he would shout the fact on the floor of the Senate, claiming that R.F.C. was inflicting a loss on the government to serve the special interests of Henry Ford and other important industrial concerns.

And in Detroit, Mr. Chrysler informed me that Mr. Ford had stated he would not in any circumstances throw any more money into the situation. Mr. Ford in the past had contributed an aggregate of $12 million to the Guardian Union Trust Company, virtually as gifts, by cancellation of deposit balances and in other ways. In addition, Mr. Ford had $7.5 million at the time in a deposit account with the bank. (Neither GM nor Chrysler had an account in the bank.)

> *Mr. Kanzler made it clear that we were expected to lend $6 million unsecured . . . the fresh money put in by us to rank parallel to the $7.5 million which Mr. Ford already had on balance. Mr. Chrysler and I had agreed before the meeting that we should insist that Mr. Ford subordinate his $7.5 million before we would extend unsecured loans, and that furthermore Mr. Ford should be called upon to share in the additional loan of $6 million that appeared to be necessary. Mr. Chrysler and I also had agreed that since the loan of fresh money was seriously important from the standpoint of serving a national public good, aid should be rendered completely by R.F.C., and that we as individual depositors in other Detroit banks should not be called upon for abnormal assistance. If the situation were bolstered by R.F.C., we would have been willing to stand by the ship, refraining from any important disturbances of our balances in other important Detroit banks.*
>
> *Mr. Chrysler and I both expressed our views, quite strongly. From equitable consideration, we should not be expected to come along with hard cash in a subordinate position. But we left the clear inference that we would bow to the limitations imposed by R.F.C., and would share in the loan of $6 million, provided that Mr. Ford would subordinate his $7.5 million already in, and provided a real effort was made to get him in addition to participate with us in the loan.*

The meeting over, Mr. Chrysler and I, with others conferred with Paul K. McKee, a national bank examiner (later a member of the Federal Reserve Board) and Arthur Ballantine, the Under Secretary of the Treasury, who made it very plain there was no chance of getting R.F.C. to go beyond $37 million. The limitation obviously was due to fear of the political consequences in the event a loan was extended which would not meet the acid test of Senator Couzen's objections.

We were in frequent contact with Messrs. Colt and Traylor, on whom we were dependent for competent analysis of the situation. The Guardian Union Trust Company was clearly insolvent; the possibility was suggested that it should be abandoned, with no attempt to reopen it on Tuesday. That would require a bolstering of the Guardian National Bank of Commerce and other units of the group to enable them to withstand the shock consequent upon suspension of business by the Trust Company. Then came still more shock:

Mr. Traylor said that before coming to any conclusion as to what should be done with respect to the Guardian group, it was important to gain a size-up of the situation at the First National Bank, so as to be satisfied there would be no danger of that bank being unable to weather the storm in the event of suspension of Guardian Union Trust. Traylor and others met for about two hours with Mr. Wilson Mills, head of the First National Bank. Following this conference, Traylor told me the condition of the First National Bank was unbelievably bad, and that it could not possibly stand up under the strain. Mills persisted that his bank was thoroughly capable of taking care of itself . . . Traylor said he was entirely unable to get Mills to recognize the facts of the situation. I accepted the opinion of Traylor, concurred in by Sloane Colt, that it would be futile to throw good money into the Guardian situation in the face of what seemed to be an assured fact that the First National Bank, unprepared to cope with the situation facing it, would fall in a short space of time.

Thus, during the day it became apparent that protection of the First National Bank, as well as the Guardian Group, would be necessary to safeguard against failures in Detroit which would lead to most serious repercussions in other parts of the country.

In the late afternoon, therefore, there was a general agreement that a rescue program in respect to the Guardian Group alone was not justified, and so as a final alternative it was determined to urge upon the Governor the extraordinary course of a banking holiday in the State of Michigan for one week. It was declared. I was informed, as further evidence of the attitude of Mr. Mills toward the situation, that he persistently refused to join with the others in the request to the Governor for the holiday.

During the course of the day I was in frequent telephone communication with Mr. Sloan, in New York. Also talked once or twice with Mr. Whitney. I explained to both of them how I had been informed that both banks actually were insolvent, and that under the circumstances there seemed to remain no alternative but the bank holiday, which would afford time to deal with the problem more deliberately and intelligently. I felt the matter to be so serious that in talking with Mr. Sloan on the phone I urged that either he stay in New York and I in Detroit, or else he come to Detroit that night, and I would go to New York, so we could gain the benefit of the best counsel and guidance from bankers in New York. It was finally determined that he would leave for Detroit and I would return to New York, arrangements being made for me to meet with Mr. Whitney immediately upon my arrival Tuesday morning.

The decision to recommend a bank holiday in Michigan established a precedent which a few weeks later was followed on a nation-wide scale. Early in the morning of March 6, newly-inaugurated President Roosevelt proclaimed a national bank holiday. The circumstances throughout the country were much the same as in Michigan, and the factors leading up to the proclamation were similar to those which had prompted the action in Michigan. President Roosevelt later wrote:

"I issued a proclamation at 1 o'clock in the morning of March 6 declaring a national bank holiday to the date set for the commencing of Congress in extraordinary session. The purpose of the closing of the banks at this time was to prevent runs which would enable one depositor to obtain an unfair advantage over another; to permit the reopening of all sound banks in an orderly manner; to keep closed the many banks which were insolvent; to permit their liquidation in a just and orderly fashion, and to permit a resumption of banking under circumstances which would instill confidence in the people as to the solvency of their banking system."

Meanwhile, in Michigan one of the big difficulties in coping with the situation was the lack of cooperative spirit between the two important banking groups in Detroit. There appeared to be a lack of leadership capable of gaining the necessary agreement upon a constructive course of action. Mr. Sloan had dinner with the Mayor of Detroit the first evening after his arrival, and later that night called me at home, urging that John Thomas Smith and I come out to Detroit immediately and try to take hold of the problem.

It was too late for a train that night, and the planes were not flying the next morning because of weather. This turned out to be beneficial because during the day, in conferences with Messrs. Gilbert, Leffingwell and others at J. P. Morgan & Co. (Mr. Whitney being in Washington that day on other matters), arrangements were made for George W. Davison, president of the Hanover National Bank of New York, to be in Detroit the next morning. I was informed that there could be no better man on whom to depend for a diagnosis of the situation and suggestions for a sound plan of attack.

Smith and I proceeded to Detroit that night. On Thursday we went first to GM building to confer with Mr. Sloan, after which the three of us went to the Detroit Club where we met Chrysler and Hutchinson, and where we proceeded to get in touch with the situation. Later in the day we saw Davison, who in the meantime had talked with Kanzler and others representing the Guardian Group, as well as Wilson Mills, representing the First National Bank. Having been brought up to date on the situation before leaving New York, Davison was able to arrive quickly at a diagnosis and on that first afternoon he suggested a concrete plan to be pursued by both banks.

Davison's plan called for creating either one or two new banks with fresh capital which would acquire from the First National and the Guardian National all of the cash and government bonds available, and in consideration therefore to assume a corresponding share of the deposit liabilities, ratably apportioned with respect to the net deposits of each institution.

Davison succeeded in bringing Mills around to a realization of the necessities of the situation, and appeared to have obtained acquiescence to the plan of reorganization. He found it more difficult to gain cooperation from the Guardian Group.

Before Mills could get the approval for the plan from his Board, three of the Directors appeared before Messrs. Sloan, Chrysler, Hutchinson, Smith and myself to object to the Davison proposal. They were unwilling to suspend operations of the First National Bank, which they said enjoyed a high standing in the community and enormous good will of depositors and other clients. They urged that the First National be allowed to reopen after the holiday, on the theory that a large number of important deposits could be subordinated, which with assistance from R.F.C. would place the institution in an invulnerable position.

We had been informed that the bank was insolvent, and did not see how we could justify the subordination of our deposits, which would have meant merely a sacrifice of our equity to the extent of capital deficiency.

We told them we had no direct knowledge of the true relationship of assets and liabilities, but that based upon such information as we had, and relying upon the advice and guidance upon which we were dependent, we could not see how the conditions could justify what would virtually amount to a contribution of capital on our part, with nothing approaching a suitable equity. We discussed the matter at some length, after which we were informed they voted in favor of the Davison plan.

Before Davison left Detroit on Friday evening, the First National Bank appeared to have agreed firmly with his plan. The Guardian *Group* had not reached a definite decision and apparently was seeking other solutions. Kanzler did indicate to us that if they could not develop some other idea, the Davison plan would be the only alternative. The Guardian Group was not very cooperative with us, and during most of the remaining days of this mission we concentrated our energies on facilitating the reorganization of the First National Bank, believing that if such a plan were perfected it would be followed by similar action or at least duplicated in principle by the Guardian National Bank of Commerce.

The Davison plan had two important objectives: first, the freeing of deposits to the greatest extent possible, ratably and without preference; and secondly, the creation of a new bank suitably capitalized and capable of providing the normal banking facilities essential to the community. As important depositors, we held that we were just as importantly concerned with the second objective as with the first, and we urged the importance of a suitable capital position for the new bank, i.e., an adequate capital ratio as between capital and deposits, and freedom from any involvement as between the new bank and the old institution.

Adapting the Davison plan, we offered for Mills' consideration the following concrete proposition:

That the old bank should borrow from R.F.C. and from other sources the maximum amount which could be procured on the basis of loans secured by assets other than cash and government bonds. Following such loan arrangements, the aggregate cash and government bonds be made available ratably to existing depositors (on the basis of net deposits without preference) through the transfer to a new bank. Such new bank would assume deposit liabilities exactly corresponding to the cash received by it from the old bank, and subject to the condition that each depositor so assenting would be required to accept a conversion of 12 per cent of the freed balance into capital stock of the new bank. The balance of 88 per cent would be payable to the depositor in cash or held for his account.

We proposed furthermore that the larger depositors, including ourselves, should subscribe to a fund which would be used for the purpose of accepting offerings of stock in the new bank for small depositors. The aggregate amount subscribed to this fund (to bail out the small depositors), together with an analysis of the small depositors' accounts, would determine the point below which, in terms of net deposits, the small depositor would have the opportunity of realizing immediately upon the required initial investment in stock of the new bank.

Assuming that loans would be derived from R.F.C. enabling the freeing of 50 per cent of the net deposit balance of the old institution, we proposed to subscribe without qualification to capital stock in the new bank equivalent to six per cent of the net balance in the old institution and that in addition we would subscribe to the fund for the purpose of accepting offerings of stock from the small depositors to the extent of four per cent of the net balance in the old institution.

Depositors representing something like $30 million of net deposits in the bank held a meeting on Saturday, February 18, and in general manifested a willingness to subscribe to capital stock of the proposed new bank to the extent of 10 per cent of the net deposits in the old institution. However, there was introduced at this meeting an insistent note by E. D. Stair, owner of the Detroit Free Press, E. R. Clark, and one or two others, that any subscribers to capital stock in the new bank should extend to the Detroit Bankers Company (a holding company holding all of the stock of First National as well as other constituent units of the Bankers' Company group) a two or three-year option to purchase the stock at cost plus six per cent interest, less any dividends which might have been received.

This requirement would have militated seriously against the new bank by denying it opportunity to gain capital subscriptions. Thus, it would have defeated to a serious degree the important objective of supplying new banking facilities to serve the community.

I arose in the meeting to say that I had every sympathy with the desire to confer every reasonable consideration and possible benefits to the former group of owners of the First National Bank, but that as depositors those of us present representing General Motors were more interested in the reestablishment of banking facilities than we were in the immediate release of a substantial part of the existing balance. Because of this primary consideration, we could not acquiesce in a plan the conditions of which would necessarily militate importantly against the procurement of fresh capital to meet continuing needs.

While, therefore, we ourselves would be perfectly content to extend an option for a reasonable period of time upon such stock as we might ourselves subscribe to, we could not consent to a program of making it obligatory on other prospective subscribers to grant similar options.

In a private discussion after the meeting with Stair and others, I elaborated my views. Stair maintained the position that unless such an option were extended the deal would be interpreted by the Detroit public as a plan to freeze out the former stockholders of the Detroit Bankers Company. I said that such misinterpretation of intentions could be dispelled if we and other participating depositors extended an option voluntarily.

After many more such hitches, and numerous conferences, subscription agreements to stock of the proposed new bank were presented to depositors of the First National Bank at a meeting on Saturday morning, February 25.

Mills was not present, the depositors' meeting having been presided over by a Mr. Sweeney, with the assistance of Mr. Long, counsel for the bank. As the meeting broke up I heard several present commenting on Mills' absence, saying, in effect, that there could hardly have been a meeting of more importance to the bank than this particular meeting of stockholders.

On the same morning, stockholders of the Guardian bank signed up subscription agreements to the capital stock of a proposed new bank in that institution, along lines identical with the First National Bank plan.

That afternoon Hutchinson and I found Mills in the R.F.C. office, in extended discussion with Washington as to the amount of loans which would be available. He was greatly discouraged, not knowing definitely about the loans, nor the amount of capital that would be required by the Comptroller of the Currency.

In New York the next day Messrs. Sloan, Chrysler, Smith, Kelly and I met at lunch with George Whitney, who extended his good offices in further communication with Washington, trying to speed up consideration of the plan we had been working on.

The next morning we awoke to find mention in the newspapers that Mr. Ford had stepped into the situation with the promise to form new banks himself, putting his own capital in without any requirements of participation by others.

It was at this point, back in New York during a "breathing spell," that I dictated the long diary. But the problem was far from solved. The relief hoped for from the newspaper accounts of Mr. Ford's entry into the picture was not forthcoming. I was called back to the scene, and spent weeks more in Detroit and in Washington. Many meetings were held among important interests dependent upon restored banking facilities to serve essential needs of the community. But the First National Bank remained closed, and none of us, as depositors, presumed to express an opinion as to whether it should be allowed to open its doors for business. We left that strictly in the hands of the national banking authorities.

By this time we were reaching the end of the Hoover

administration, with Franklin D. Roosevelt assuming his first term of office in March. After preliminary meetings with the Comptroller of the Currency and the Secretary of the Treasury, I engaged in extended discussions with Jesse Jones, head of R.F.C., which resulted in negotiations on a new plan whereby General Motors Corporation would set up a new bank in Detroit, with aid from R.F.C. The institution, to be known as the National Bank of Detroit, would take over liquid and sound assets from the closed First National. GM stood ready to underwrite $12.5 million of common stock to be issued, and R.F.C. agreed to subscribe a like amount of preferred stock to be issued. With approval of the Treasury Department, and with firm acquiescence by R.F.C., we insisted that mortgages to be transferred to the new bank could not exceed in the aggregate $25 million, representing the total contemplated paid-in capital, and also that mortgages taken over would be carefully selected and subject in each instance to close analysis as to soundness. As I recollect, the closed bank held mortgages aggregating something like $170 million.

Another condition we insisted upon was that GM's role was that of underwriter, with the stock initially subscribed by us to be offered to depositors and stockholders of the closed institution under a designated apportionment, at cost price per share.

These conditions were arrived at through extended discussions with the Comptroller of the Currency, in conjunction with the R.F.C. The limitations as to selection of mortgages, and the taking over of other sound banking assets with appropriate assumption of liability to depositors, were not only agreed to by them; actually, they insisted upon them.

With these basic points agreed, it then rested upon us to undertake the preliminary steps necessary to actual creation of the new bank. In this we were assisted on the ground in Detroit by Ned Potter, of the Guarantee Trust Company of New York, who was recommended by New York advisors. Potter, John Thomas Smith and I spent days canvassing the field for the best qualified man to head up the new institution as president. We also concerned ourselves with the need to find suitable citizens of Michigan who would be ready to accept directorships. In this we were successful, gaining acceptance from each person approached, and a good representative group was assured. In addition to these, Smith and I were to assume directorship, together with Stanley Reed, then general counsel of R.F.C., as representing its interests.

Examining the possibilities as to the presidency, we ruled out the idea of finding the right person among the bankers of Detroit. The man settled upon as the most desirable choice was Walter McLucas, who had distinguished himself as a person of high competency in service as one of the top executives in the Commerce Trust Company of Kansas City. He accepted our invitation to visit Detroit, and after a day with Smith, Potter, and me, agreed to give the matter serious thought. McLucas said that if he were to accept the post, he would want to bring along with him two or three men from his staff in Kansas City; to this we agreed. Soon afterward, McLucas communicated his willingness to accept the job. We had an informal meeting with the group that was to constitute the directorship, which gave approval.

The National Bank of Detroit was then formally created, and a date was set to open the doors for business. At this point, a great hue and cry had arisen in Detroit, inspired largely by Police Commissioner Watkins, to the effect that GM's intercession in the banking situation was "robbing the former stockholders and others of their rights." Statements were published that the depositors of the closed bank, in receivership, would not have full access to deposits standing to their credit. (GM and other large depositors actually had agreed to subordinate their claims to an extent favoring transfer of deposit accounts to the new bank in behalf of small depositors, thus rendering their claims liquid.)

McLucas was delayed for some days in attending to affairs connected with his separation from the Kansas City institution, and arrived in Detroit on the afternoon of the day on which the new bank opened. A formal meeting of the Board was convened. A majority of the directors present insisted that the National Bank of Detroit should take over all of the mortgages held by the defunct institution. This was completely unanticipated. McLucas, familiar with the conditions under which the new bank had been created, and by reason, too, of his own sound concepts of banking procedure, was profoundly shocked. The meeting closed without definite action, and McLucas, Smith, Reed and I went into an almost all-night session to cope with the problem. Reed was in constant communication with his superior, Jesse Jones, who put all the pressure he could upon us to accede to the majority view of the Board.

Finally, I had to put it that the limitations with respect to assumption of mortgages had been solidly agreed to by R.F.C. as well as by the Comptroller of the Currency, and that it was only on this basis that GM had accepted the role of sponsorship of the new bank. I put it further that if the basic principle were to be abrogated, GM would withdraw its capital contribution, and leave it to R.F.C. and others to provide the funds necessary to restore sound banking facilities to Detroit. The opposing forces came to withdraw opposition, and the National Bank of Detroit continued in business, and has been successful over succeeding years, enjoying during McLucas' lifetime the benefit of his effective leadership.

So much for the bank holiday and its strenuous aftermath. But this story has a sequel. Some months later I was cruising on a yacht in the Potomac River waters. Mrs. Brown and I had a group of friends on board, and one Sunday we invited Mr. and Mrs. Jones and Mr. and Mrs. Reed to come along for an all-day cruise, which was a very pleasant one.

During the afternoon, Jones said in a private conversation with me, referring to the controversy about the mortgages: "Thank God, you stood by your guns!" General Motors had taken the grief, and had relieved R.F.C. from the necessity of appearing in an unpopular light. I'm sure that on the night when he was intensely "putting the heat" on us to give in to the misguided public clamor, Jesse Jones was counting on our standing fast on the settled agreement.

It was an example of the sort of thing I have seen on a number of occasions; i.e., an individual in public office appears in the light of favoring public opinion of the moment, contrary to his inner convictions. Off the record, he is depending upon private parties concerned to stand firm on the ground of sound procedure. The official may not be free, because of political exigency or the dictum of a superior, to apply his own best judgment. There is little to be gained in deploring such a situation; the important point is to recognize it.

2. *The Blue Eagle and Labor Relations.*

Soon after President Roosevelt's "New Deal" administration took over in Washington, the Congress enacted the National Industrial Recovery Act, commonly known as N.R.A. It came to be known even more widely later as the "Blue Eagle," because of the colorful emblem it adopted for identification purposes. The N.R.A. also had a colorful personality as its administrator, General Hugh (Iron Pants) Johnson. A few years later, the Act was to be declared unconstitutional by the U. S. Supreme Court, and still later, addressing the Congress in 1937, President Roosevelt admitted that "in sober second thought," its difficulties arose "from the fact that it tried to do too much."

The N.R.A. was designed to do two things: First, to remove some of the legal restrictions of the anti-trust laws, permitting certain areas of collaboration among industrial units engaged in specific fields; and second, to promote the aspirations of organized labor. The latter objective was recognized in the famous Section 7 (a) of the law, which extended the right to employees to organize and bargain collectively through representatives of their own choosing. The Act contained a provision, too, that no employee be required, as a condition of employment, to join any company union, or to refrain from joining, organizing or assisting a labor organization of his own choosing.

The Act provided that business and industry could come under the cloak of the law by voluntary subscription to an "industry code," and the automotive industry, represented then by what was known as the National Automobile Chamber of Commerce (now the Automobile Manufacturers Association) took this question under consideration. I was appointed Chairman of an Industry Committee to handle the matter. The Ford Motor Company was not then a member of the N.A.A.C. (Ford joined the industry association in the summer of 1955), but in this particular case representatives of Ford were named to the special committee and sat in all of its meetings. Other members represented virtually all companies in the automotive industry.

Meetings extended over a number of weeks, after which a decision was reached to sign up. But at this point, Mr. Ford elected to withdraw, and remained steadfast in his unwillingness to subscribe to the industry's course of action.

The industry's decision to sign up under N.R.A. was based solely on its readiness to submit to the requirements of Section 7 (a). The committee unanimously rejected the opportunity offered by the law to seek any relief from existing anti-trust statutes, and in public appearances before the N.R.A. in Washington, as representative of the industry, I made this point amply clear. Incidentally, the position of the industry (excluding Ford) on the whole N.R.A. matter had the full approval of GM executives concerned with corporation policy, with whom I had numerous conferences during the deliberations of the industry committee.

Subsequently, the N.R.A. became the channel through which the American Federation of Labor demanded industry-wide bargaining, and amid threats of a strike in the automobile industry, extended negotiations eventually were undertaken, with General Johnson, head of N.R.A. in charge. I participated in the negotiations, serving as chief spokesman for the industry. Among others representing the industry were Walter Chrysler, B. E. Hutchinson and Nicholas Kelly, of Chrysler; Alvan MacCauley, head of Packard Motor Car Company and President of the

N.A.C.C.; Charles W. Nash, of the Nash Motor Company, and John Thomas Smith, GM General Counsel.

We maintained that the A.F. of L. was not qualified to bargain in behalf of employees of the industry, the law did not require it, and therefore we refused to negotiate directly with representatives of that organization. We had many sessions with General Johnson, and several with President Roosevelt. Often, meeting in N.R.A. headquarters, we would sit in one room while William Green, head of the A.F. of L., and his associates would sit in an adjoining room, with the General and his aides shuttling back and forth in an effort to bring about some kind of reconciliation.

The issues were serious and there were many moments of tension. But there were some light and pleasant interludes, as well, to relieve the strain. One of these grew out of an early visit with the President. It was common knowledge at the time that the administration in Washington was keenly resentful when industry or banking interests brought legal counsel into negotiations with government agencies.

On this particular occasion, I was acting as spokesman for the automotive group. As the session broke up, President Roosevelt asked me point blank whether I was a lawyer. I was able to assure the President of my innocence in that regard, so the subject was not pursued in the White House. But it was taken up again, with gleeful vengeance, when our delegation got back to our quarters in the hotel. There was much joshing back and forth, Walter Chrysler in his jovial way insisting that I had been revealed as a "Harvard pink." Everybody enjoyed the fun as we waited for the next round.

After prolonged negotiations, we drew up a statement of principles which incorporated the fundamental position of the industry. General Johnson approved it and then obtained its acceptance by the A.F. of L. We then went with the General to present the case to the President. In this session, Mr. Roosevelt not only embraced the principles on which we had stood, but actually changed phrasing in the statement at one or two spots which improved the language. He immediately issued the statement to the press, describing it as the greatest forward step that had been taken in the area of labor relations.

This statement, dated March 25, 1934, covered the fundamental issue as follows:

"1. Reduced to plain language, Section 7 (a) of N.I.R.A. means:

"a) Employees have the right to organize into a group or groups.

"b) When such group or groups are organized they can choose representatives by free choice; and such representatives must be received collectively, in order to straighten out disputes and improve conditions of employment.

"c) Discrimination against employees because of their labor affiliations, or for any other unfair or unjust reason, is barred."

In an appended "statement of procedure and principles," it was agreed that N.R.A. would set up "a Board, to be known as the Automobile Labor Board, responsible to the President of the United States, to sit in Detroit to pass on all questions of representation, discharge and discrimination. Decision of the Board shall be final and binding on employer and employees. Such a board is to have access to all payrolls and to all lists of claimed employee representation, and such board will be composed of (a) a labor representative, (b) an industry representative, and (c) a neutral.

"The Government makes it clear that it favors no particular union or particular form of employee organization or representation. The Government's only duty is to secure absolute and uninfluenced freedom of choice without coercion, restraint or intimidation from any source.

"The industry understands that in reduction or increase of force, such human considerations as whether a man is married and has a family shall come first, and then seniority, individual skill and efficient service. After these factors have been considered, no greater proportion of outside union employees similarly situated shall be laid off than of other employees. By 'outside union employees' it is understood a paid-up member in good standing, or anyone legally obligated to pay up."

The President's statement described the settlement as "a framework for a new structure of industrial relations — a new basis of understanding between employers and employees."

"I would like you to know," his statement said, "that in the settlement just reached in the automobile industry we have charted a new course in social engineering in the United States. It is my hope that out of this will come a new realization of the opportunities of capital and labor not only to compose their differences at the conference table and to recognize their respective rights and responsibilities, but also to establish a foundation on which they can cooperate in bettering the human relationships involved in any large industrial enterprise."

In the light of these words of hearty endorsement, it is an ironic fact that within a year the President, confronted with pressure from organized labor opposing the principles, backed away from the agreement.

The Automobile Labor Board provided in the agreement was created and went into action immediately, conducting supervised elections, plant-by-plant. The President appointed Dr. Leo Wolman as public representative and chairman; Nicholas Kelly, general counsel of the Chrysler Corporation, was named by the automotive industry as its representative. The United Automobile Workers, which at the time was affiliated with the A.F. of L., appointed as its representative one of its officers.

The Board continued to function effectively and expeditiously for some months, in accordance with the terms of the agreement, but resistance from labor increased, and in response to the political aspects of this opposition, the President gave the project a kiss of death. The Automobile Labor Board was disbanded within a year of its establishment.

Section 7 (a) of the National Industry Recovery Act

had come into disrepute in the minds of the leaders of national organized labor who were competing among themselves for domination in collective bargaining. They resented and opposed the basic principles which were embodied in the President's settlement agreement in the automotive industry, and which shortly afterwards were contained also in a "Statement of General Motors Corporation's Basic Policies Governing Its Relations With Factory Employees." They held that collective bargaining on a local basis, with representatives of employees chosen from among themselves, was the equivalent of "company unions," subject to employer domination. The counsel and direction of "professional" labor leaders was, in their view, essential. Further, they wanted the benefits of dues-paying members of affiliated unions, looking toward the accumulation of centralized treasuries that could be put to good use, from their standpoint, for political purposes. Finally, they wanted resources available for strike funds; workers thrown out of employment by strike are more amenable to arguments in behalf of work stoppages when they are afforded some relief in meeting living costs. All of these desires conflicted with the fundamental principles of collective bargaining as set forth in the settlement President Roosevelt had achieved, and thus he became subject to great political pressures to back away from the agreement.

Under the N.R.A., the President had created the National Labor Relations Board to administer labor policies, on the theory that actual or threatened strikes impaired the nation's economic recovery. The experience in the automobile industry was one of a series of events which operated to weaken the opportunity for the NLRB to function in that manner. The terms of the settlement agreement in the automobile industry, averting an industry-wide strike, were never accepted in spirit by organized labor. The fact that the President intervened to help bring about that settlement served to further impair the efficacy of the national labor board. Finally, as pressures were brought to bear, Congress enacted in 1935 the National

Labor Relations Act, sponsored by Senator Wagner. The so-called Wagner Act has remained the law of the land, subject to qualifying features of interpretative nature — the Taft-Hartley Act — later enacted by Congress.

As mentioned above, during the period when the industry committee had the N.R.A. matter under consideration, I maintained close contact with my associates in GM, who participated in the formulation of principles which came to be accepted by other members of the industry. General Motors felt it desirable to draw up a statement of its own policies concerning labor relations, and it devolved upon me to attend to the drafting of it. The statement, which was referred to previously, was adopted after extended discussion and debate. It was approved by the Executive Committee, signed by Mr. Sloan as President, and under date of August 15, 1934, was given wide circulation to personnel throughout the organization, including factory employees.

The declaration of principles represents a sound philosophy of employer-employee relations, conforming with the law of the country then existing. It gave effect to the accepted right of employees to engage in collective bargaining through representatives of their own choosing. At the same time it held to the philosophy of collective bargaining on the local level, where there could be intimacy of association in dealing with mutual interests of employer and employee, consistent with decentralized administrative structure. Certainly the principles embodied in this document were far removed from any concept of industry-wide bargaining or national unionization. The statement is worth preserving, and is reproduced in full in the Appendix.

With the transfer of U.A.W. affiliation from the A.F. of L. to the Congress of Industrial Organizations, John L. Lewis became the power behind the throne. In 1937, the notorious sit-down strikes were called in several GM plants, through the activity of U.A.W.-C.I.O. These sit-down strikes represented the unlawful seizure of private property, and the Corporation took the firm stand that there would be no recognition of U.A.W.-C.I.O. as qualified bargaining agents so long as the seizure of GM plants continued. During this period, Mr. Lewis assumed personal leadership in seeking to open negotiations with the corporation in behalf of U.A.W.-C.I.O. General Motors refused to enter into negotiations with him, or with U.A.W.-C.I.O., so long as any of its plants remained unlawfully seized, unless commanded to do so by the highest government authority. By such authority was meant, of course, the President of the United States.

Governor Frank Murphy, of Michigan, tried in every way he could to bring us into negotiation with U.A.W.-C.I.O., and we had many sessions with the Governor, one of them in the Governor's mansion in Lansing lasting throughout an entire night. In these sessions I served as spokesman for GM, with W. S. Knudsen, then President, and John Thomas Smith, General Counsel, sitting in. During that extended night session, we sat in one room and Mr. Lewis and his associates sat in another. Our position was that when the struck plants were restored to the management, we would be willing to enter into negotiation.

When it became evident to him that he could not prevail upon us to alter our stand, Governor Murphy brought pressure on us from Washington. We had appeals from the Secretary of Labor, and direct telephone communications from the President, asking us to negotiate. We persisted in our refusal, and believed we had wide public sentiment in favor of our position.

Finally, on an evening when Messrs. Knudsen, Smith and I were in our offices in the General Motors Building, I had a call from the Governor who told me that he had received word from Washington that the President requested us to enter into negotiations with Mr. Lewis. My reply was that we would have to receive the request directly from the President, as we had reiterated many times. The Governor questioned whether the President would be willing to issue such a "command," and the matter was dropped for the moment.

After this call, we pondered the situation, and talked

several times with Mr. Sloan in New York. We accepted it that Governor Murphy had been authorized to convey the President's request, and that it was, in actuality, a command. Finally we agreed that if we could gain the President's approval to a statement which we would issue to the press, reporting his request upon us, that would fulfill the requirement of placing responsibility for our action on government.

Accordingly, we prepared such a release, it was cleared with Mr. Sloan and then I read it to Governor Murphy over the telephone, explaining it was intended for publication in the event we acceded to the President's request. The Governor said it would "put the President on a spot," and I argued that that was the only reason we could be willing to enter into negotiations, as we had made amply clear.

The Governor took down a copy of the statement, to convey to President Roosevelt, and later in the evening he telephoned back to say that the President had authorized him to tell us he sanctioned the issuance of the statement by General Motors. Thereupon, the statement was released to the press, and the next day we began negotiations with Mr. Lewis, with Governor Murphy carrying on as mediator. The struck plants were restored to management's normal jurisdiction with resumption of operations.

In contending with the problems involved in the seizure of some of the corporation's plants, and in the course of subsequent negotiation, I represented Sloan, who was the executive head of the Corporation. It was recognized that my concern was with questions related to basic policies, and that I did not serve as an expert in the field of employer-employee relations. As a result of many hours of discussion of problems in this area over the years, the executives in top management came to share basically uniform viewpoints with respect to fundamental policy. In this way, I had solid ground on which to stand in representing the corporation. The negotiations with Mr. Lewis extended over some days, resulting in an agreement as to the general basis on which further negotiations would be conducted with U.A.W.-C.I.O. insofar as they were qualified to represent employees for purposes of collective bargaining. Thereafter, the more detailed problems were taken over by the central labor relations staff, under the chief guidance of C. E. Wilson, then Executive Vice President of the Corporation.

Many people felt that we had backed down from our public pronouncement that we would not negotiate until the struck plants were restored. One of these was Senator Millard Tydings, of Maryland. Shortly after the negotiations began, I accepted an invitation to attend a meeting of the Chamber of Commerce, in Havre de Grace, Maryland. (Traveling by air, I was absent from the scene in Detroit only a short time.) At the dinner-meeting I sat next to Senator Tydings, who raked General Motors over the coals for what he called capitulating to the sit-down strikes. He contended — and we all agreed — that to submit to the pressures of an illegal strike was fraught with serious consequences, and dangerous to the economic life of the nation, and he thought that the public had strongly favored GM's refusal to enter into negotiations under the prevailing circumstances.

The Senator was familiar with the qualification which had been stated in our pronouncement; i.e., that we would accede only if commanded to do so by "the highest government authority," and he conceded that upon demand by the President we would have no alternative but to comply. But he felt that our method of complying was in error; that we should have insisted upon receiving the command directly from the President and in writing. It was his view that the general public would not realize, from the General Motors' release, that we had actually received such a request from the highest authority.

Senator Tydings may have been right. There were many others who felt the same way at the time. If we had to do it over again, maybe we would insist upon a direct command, which could be published. At the time, those of us dealing with the issue felt that such a nicety might be construed as insulting, since the President had gone so far as to sanction our release of the statement announcing his request.

Going through the memos, clippings and notes of this period, I find an amusing sidelight in a copy of NEWSWEEK magazine dated January 16, 1937. In a lengthy report on developments in the sit-down strikes against GM appears a somewhat unflattering picture of me, with this explanation: "Those close to the corporation thought a little-known, publicity-shy electrical engineer directed General Motors tactics behind the headlined names of Sloan and Knudsen." The magazine may have been correct about the degree of my prominence, but my concern was with strategy, not tactics, and I was operating at all times not as an individual but as a member of a top-level management team.

3. Declaration of Industrial Principles

Early in 1939 I was asked by the National Association of Manufacturers to take the chairmanship of what was called a "Coordinating Committee," charged with drafting a statement to be presented to the Congress of American Industry in December. This had been a customary annual event, resulting in a declaration of principles being adopted by a widely-representative assemblage of industry executives, followed by broad publication in the press. The committee over which I agreed to preside comprised 85 individuals, most of them leading industry executives.

The first meeting was held over a weekend at Absecon, N. J., with a large and interested attendance. The European war had just broken out, and while our own country was not then directly involved, it was clearly recognized that our economy at home, and the conduct of industry, inevitably would be greatly affected. I had had no previous identity with the N.A.M., but had been familiar with prior annual pronouncements emanating from the Congress, and with interim statements by N.A.M. itself. Usually, these were belligerent statements, with attacks upon governmental activities. Many of these attacks were against courses of action which obviously had preponderant public support, mistaken though the judgment of majority opinion might have been. It seemed to me that N.A.M. clearly had been resorting to pressure group tactics, presuming to speak for managers of industry; in other words, placing itself in the same kind of light as the very pressure groups which N.A.M. was condemning.

So in the course of my remarks at the Abescon meeting, I said that the need was for positive leadership by industrial executives at all levels of management.

"The Association's declaration must, if this end is to be achieved, address itself consciously and directly to the managers of industry. It must be couched in terms that will appeal to the sense of security and enlightened self-interest of industry itself. It must make it plain to industrial management that unless the things called for are done, and the responsibilities to society accepted, the people will lose their last faith in industrial leadership, and turn — as they have turned in other countries — to other leaders who offer them glittering promises and specious security.

"To me, it would seem futile for the Association to address itself directly to the public. It would seem futile to ask the public to accept the principles expounded at face value, without assurance of industry's compliance. Rather, the message must be addressed to industrial management, directly and squarely, in an effort to persuade the public indirectly, but in that way more convincingly, that they can rely upon the force of enlightened self-interest to accomplish the essentials of industrial control in the broad interests of society."

My statement was well received by a large majority of those present, but in all of the sessions of this group, as the work of drafting the statement went on, there were always voices raised against the approach I had suggested. Even in the course of the last meeting, when seeking approval of a statement which then had been developed in final form, one belligerent member offered for consideration an alternative declaration which he had carefully prepared in advance. It was more of the same old "fighting statement," the very essence of which is pressure group tactics in which the Association purports to speak for, and not to, industry. There were long arguments, but the outcome was approval by a preponderant majority of the statement we had submitted.

In December at the Congress of American Industry, the work of the Coordinating Committee was warmly applauded by the large assemblage of industrialists, and the "Declaration of Principles" was approved and given wide distribution. The statement received cordial acceptance by the press and by agencies of government. However, there still remains to this day a continuing struggle as to the sound approach which the industry association should take in public pronouncements on major issues. I think a few paragraphs from that "Declaration of Principles" of 1939, to which thousands of industrialists pledged support, are worth reprinting here:

"The American people have faith in constitutional representative democracy, in free enterprise, and in civil and religious liberty, as inseparable fundamentals of freedom to be cherished and preserved. These fundamentals have made possible the development of our natural and human resources, and have resulted in the greatest degree of personal freedom, the widest opportunity, and the highest standard of living in all the world.

"The Congress of American Industry, convinced that a system of free enterprise is essential to America's greatness, calls upon the managers of industry to continue to do their part in assuring the fruits of that system to the American people. It calls upon them to serve the enlightened interests of industry itself by serving the interests of the nation as a whole.

"The American citizen wants an opportunity to earn the necessities of life, and the comforts and luxuries that go to make life richer — not only material necessities, but also the opportunity to enjoy cultural and spiritual satisfaction. He wants to feel secure — in his liberties and for his person, in his job and for his old age, in himself and for his family.

"The achievements of American industry command the admiration of the civilized world. These achievements derive from a system of free enterprise founded upon the bedrock of constitutional government designed to protect the individual in his right to life, liberty, and the pursuit of happiness . . . In contrast to the American system stands planned economy — the system employed in every totalitarian state. Political dictatorship, on which this alien system is based, is repellent to Americans because it destroys personal liberty, religious freedom and individual initiative.

"Industry's contribution to the national security and welfare, in common with that of the other elements of private enterprise, must be made within a system of laws enacted under the authority of the people, and administered by government. Government, in the broad interests of society, must be one of law, and not of men. It must be guided by established principles — not by arbitrary action. Regulations thus provided should be designed to stimulate, and not to stifle, the efforts which are made by all elements of the national economy, including industry, to pursue their legitimate ends . . . . .

"It is in the sphere of its own immediate activity that the challenge to industrial management lies . . . . . The managers of industry must continue unabated their efforts in behalf of increased production and employment, with ever-increasing realization of the contribution this effort can make to national unity and security. This requires an application by industrial management of policies basic to the welfare of industry as a whole, and to the broader welfare of the nation. Good management will recognize that it serves its own interests best as it strives to serve also the interests of the nation as a whole."

4. *Analyzing Social and Economic Trends*

I have before me as I write this a 4,000-word memorandum written by me to Mr. Sloan on June 22, 1938, on the subject of "Policy Group — Economic and Social Trends." The memorandum documented in considerable detail the fact that rapid changes were occurring in social and economic conditions, requiring a continual adjustment of corporation policies, organization attitudes and management technique. It led to the establishment of a policy group devoted to these broad problems.

Much of the change, of course, directly stemmed from political actions. These in turn resulted from the pressures of public opinion, and as we viewed them the trends represented marked departures from allegiance to the fundamental principles essential to maintenance of a free and competitive economy.

Giving increasing attention to these broad problems, I was concerned not only with making sure they were understood but also, and very importantly, that their effects were carefully projected. Whether we liked them or not, such trends obviously were destined to have major impact upon the conduct of business, and hence must be realistically appraised. A primary responsibility of the proposed policy group would be to develop such information on a reliable basis for the general guidance of the corporation management.

Although much of the subject matter necessarily would be in the realm of government and politics, we did not wish to use either of those words, lest the purpose of the activity be misconstrued. There was no intent to engage in lobbying activities of any kind. So the title given was "Policy Group — Social and Economic Trends," and I was named Chairman. The group met each month, functioning in conformance with the purposes I have previously mentioned, until we became involved in World War II. Under the conditions of war-time regimentation which then arose, normal and desirable relationships between industry and government necessarily were suspended. The activities of this particular group were halted, as also were those of other policy groups in GM which had concerned themselves with problems of corporation planning and coordinated control.

CHAPTER VII

War, Post-War and Retirement

In 1940, President Roosevelt made direct overtures to Bill Knudsen to become head of the nation's defense production program. Knudsen had been serving very effectively as President of General Motors, and all of us hated to see him enter the maelstrom of Washington. He was a wonderful operator, and we felt he could render a greater service to his country by remaining with GM.

Bill Knudsen had a marked appreciation of the requirements of coordinated control, and of the need for administration to conform to basic policies, as these policies evolved and won acceptance. He and I worked wonderfully in harness. With his great gift of homely expression, he used to make the point himself by saying: "There are two kinds of people needed in management, the 'thinker-upper' and the 'getter-doner.'"

Despite all of our persuasive force, we were unable to convince Mr. Knudsen that he should refuse the President's request. He took it as a command. This country had made him, he said, and when he had a call from the government of his country, he was not going to refuse. So he left General Motors and went to Washington, to head up the Office of Production Management, as the agency was then known. (Later it had several other names, finally became the War Production Board.)

Arriving in the capital, Knudsen surely must have had misgivings when the President insisted that the agency be headed by two men — William Knudsen for industry and Sidney Hillman for labor. But when I saw Bill from time to time he loyally insisted that he and Hillman were "getting along fine."

In time, however, Mr. Knudsen suffered a tremendous shock. This was when he learned that he was being removed from his defense production job, to be made a lieutenant general of the Army, with an assignment to expedite production. He wasn't given the courtesy of receiving this news from the President who had summoned him to Washington; he got it from a friend, "Tommy" Thompkins (L. D. Thompkins of U.S. Rubber), who had read it on a news ticker. I happened to be in Washington that day on other business, and had a dinner date with Knudsen, so I called at his office. He drove me to his home; a couple of other friends were present, and it was a distressing evening because of the heartbreak we knew Bill Knudsen was suffering.

Meanwhile, back in Detroit, C. E. Wilson, who had served as Executive Vice President since the 1937 reorganization, succeeded Knudsen as GM President. A man of great vision and competence, Wilson was a quite different type of operator from Knudsen. He accepted the responsibilities of the presidency as seriously as could have been wished for by all concerned; he displayed imagination, and a firm grasp of operating phases. At the same time, Wilson felt immediate concern over questions of policy, and unlike his predecessor in the presidency, sometimes was impatient with the delays which were necessary for consideration of issues in New York, and for the thorough orientation of all personnel in agreed-upon policies before they were laid down as rules of procedure.

To understand the change which gradually took place in this regard during Wilson's presidency, it is necessary to know something of the background. Always, many problems of management are of such a character as to render difficult a clear demarcation between considerations of a pure financial nature and those relating to actual operations. Because of this, the reorganization of 1937 consolidated the functions previously resting upon the dual committees, Finance and Executive, into a central Policy Committee. During the succeeding 10 years, with the Policy Committee serving as the governing body, and with Sloan continuing his headquarters in New York and the President headquartered in Detroit, those with managerial responsibilities in the corporation came to look upon "New

York" as the seat of policy formulation and "Detroit" as the seat of management direction.

But while "New York" was considered the seat of policy making, it did not follow that those headquartered there had any feeling of self-sufficiency in dealing with questions of fundamental policy. On the contrary, great care was taken to assure "two-way communication" up and down the organization, so that there would be free and open discussion of every issue, and further to assure that once a given course of procedure was decided upon there would be a complete orientation among GM personnel. It is essential that those with administrative responsibilities accept each point of policy, fully appreciate it, and thus be able to effectuate it in the spirit and purpose intended.

To this end Policy Groups were designated (and still function) to give attention to policy considerations in each major sphere of corporate interest. Each group was equipped with staff, located in Detroit, and maintained close contact and collaboration with operating executives, including group executives, general managers of divisions, and junior personnel. "New York" maintained representation on these groups, and frequent meetings were held, with elaborate presentations, to make sure that the final result would contribute to more effective coordinated control. These groups had no authority in policy formulation. Frequently, the operating executives directly concerned would be brought in afterwards for seminar discussions of the issues involved, and sometimes similar discussions were also conducted within the Administration Committee. Every effort was made to indoctrinate the entire organization. This proved so successful that most policies were arrived at, and implemented, without the necessity of any formal action, either by the Executive Committee, in the earlier years, or by the Policy Committee during the years 1937 to 1946. Only matters of broadest import had to be resolved by the top policy echelon during that period.

This situation prevailed during those years when Alfred P. Sloan was serving as the Chief Executive Officer. Because of his grasp of the operating problems of the corporation, it was perfectly natural, in the 1937 reorganization, for him to remain as both Chairman and executive head of the corporation. First Bill Knudsen, and later C. E. Wilson, had to accept the logic of his position as their superior. But in 1946, when Mr. Sloan retired from active duty, the basic situation assumed a quite different complexion. It was apparent to everyone that no one was qualified to function in New York both as Chairman of the Board and Chief Executive Officer.

So at that time there was a major change; the President was constituted the Chief Executive Officer, accountable to the governing committees. The Chairman of the Financial Policy Committee had no executive duties, as such. True, this individual had administrative jurisdiction over the Financial and Legal departments, and the Finance and Insurance groups. But in that capacity, he carried the title of Executive Vice President, and therefore was subject, at least by implication, to the President. In the organization chart, to be sure, a dotted line from the President to this particular Executive Vice President suggested a measure of independence. But in practice it seems fair to say that this independence did not exist to the degree which would be wholesome and beneficial. It is quite likely that if the Chairman of the Financial Policy Committee (or Finance Committee) were to relinquish his executive responsibilities, there could be restored to much better effect the objectivity of treatment and wise counsel on matters of coordinated control, so important to the long-range welfare of the corporation.

This type of corporate management obviously requires delay in the determination and the dissemination of basic policy. It was this delay which bothered Wilson. I continued through his regime as representative of Mr. Sloan, the chief executive officer, in matters of labor relations, government relations and other areas as specifically assigned. In serving under such assigned duties, I always was most careful to make sure my line of attack was in accord with Sloan's concepts, and with the settled fundamental policy of the corporation. By early 1946, Wilson had come to feel that his courses of action in coping with vital problems of the business were restricted, and his effectiveness handicapped, by the requirement of bowing to "New York." He used to say to me, in the friendliest of terms, that it was "damned difficult to serve two masters." I could have sympathy with that viewpoint, but so long as I was a part of the "New York" policy-making group, I could not bow to the theory of subordinating the top level objectives of the corporation — the primary basic aims — to administrative exigencies. To do so would, in my judgment, contribute toward the development within the corporation of something in the nature of a "dictatorship," which would bode no good for the future interests of the stockholders.

Then, early in 1946, Sloan determined upon the idea of relinquishing the arduous duties of chief executive officer, reestablishing the previous dual committee governing structure, and transferring the chief executive responsibilities to Detroit. During the early stages of his consideration of this change, Sloan asked me whether I would be willing to assume the Chairmanship of the Board. I told him that I would consider it if it would call for my full time, with continued intimacy of contact with Detroit. Further, I felt that the Financial and Public Relations departments should remain under the jurisdiction of the Chairman. It was my belief that there was no necessity for the President to report to the Chairman; on the contrary, I would not be interested in assuming the duties of Chief Executive Officer. Sloan agreed with my suggestions, both of us feeling that the contemplated form of organization would serve to an important degree in preserving the values of "New York's" objectivity of treatment with regard to fundamental policy considerations. I communicated with Lammot duPont and Walter Carpenter, who were vacationing at the time in Florida. Both registered approval of the arrangement upon which Sloan and I had agreed. After consulting with Mrs. Brown, I told Sloan that I would be ready to take on the job. Then I took off for a winter vacation in Hot Spring, Virginia.

I returned to my New York office shortly before the reorganization plan was to be placed before the Board for action. Then I found that Wilson and others had prevailed upon Mr. Sloan to carry on as Chairman of the Board, free from executive duties. I was invited to accept the position of a new committee to be created — Financial Policy Committee. This did not appeal to me, inasmuch as I had already formed some ideas of how I could advance my personal plans and ambitions, once retired from active duty with GM. Besides this, I knew that Albert Bradley was highly qualified to fill the Chairmanship of this proposed committee; more effectively, in fact, than could I, in view of the plan for the top organizational set-up.

So I elected to retire from active duty, but remained on the Board, and on the Financial Policy Committee. The retirement I speak of occurred in June, 1946. I had long preached the doctrine under which those in supervisory positions should strive to work themselves out of jobs through the training of competent successors. In stepping aside, a few years before the statutory age of retirement, I became a "victim" of my own doctrinaire!

But with no anguishing regrets.

BUSINESS ASSOCIATES OVER THE YEARS. L. to R., E. F. Johnson, W. F. Harrington, John L. Pratt. I consider John Pratt to be my oldest and best friend.

CHAPTER VIII

Looking Ahead

Through the years I have shared with my business associates a firm belief in the fundamental principles of the form of government under which we have been privileged to live, and also in what is commonly referred to as the free competitive enterprise system. Consequently, the trends we have witnessed toward socialism, evidenced by measures symbolic of the "welfare state," have been disconcerting, to say the least. Some of these measures, indeed, have been downright shocking to those who hold solidly, as I do, to faith in the good will and common sense of the American people.

Such trends, I have come to believe, are derived largely from political interpretation of "public pressures" which have been mobilized by the aspiring leaders of pressure groups of various kinds, seeking selfish ends, and fanned into exaggeration by their unwitting allies, the well-intentioned but misguided "do-gooders." In the emotional fervor of a "cause," it is easy for the individual to forget that each citizen is dependent upon the welfare of all, and that the common welfare depends in turn upon the service of each individual of his own interest through service to society.

Many blame the politicians for these departures from sound fundamental concepts, asserting that those in public office are inclined to cater to the whims and fancies of transitory public opinion, or to the desires and aspirations of group leaders in various fields of governmental concern. Very often such blame is misplaced. There are inescapable limitations upon the person in public office as to how far he can go, in exercising true statesmanship, to buck the tide of public opinion, however uninformed and mistaken that opinion may be. Often the right-minded man in public office can serve his country best by biding his time, allowing opportunity for the true facts of a situation to bring enlightenment to bear upon the voting constituents to whom he is accountable. Better this than to have this person thrown out of authority, to be replaced by another official who is merely riding the waves of transitory popularity.

My personal impulse is to rebel immediately against any statement or action which seems to lack allegiance to the principles which form the basic foundation to our society. Yet here, too, it is well to "make haste slowly"; to withhold criticism on specific issues until one can be absolutely sure of his ground. Often when such circumstances arise, I have to stop and ponder, remembering that an individual on the outside does not always have complete familiarity with all of the pros and cons of the specific issues involved.

A good example of this came shortly after the turn of the century when the Sherman anti-trust law was proposed, supplemented by the Clayton Act. I am sure that the citizens of that day holding basic beliefs such as mine heartily resented the government's procedure. Yet today, like-minded individuals completely accept those laws as being necessary for the public good. How much better off we are than if government had left the door open to cartelization within industry, such as has wrought so much harm to the British economy!

Throughout my business life, up to my retirement in 1946, I never had the time to be a stock market operator, entirely apart from disinclination and ineptness. Instead, I endeavored constantly to accumulate available excess income for investment, and as noted previously, made progressive investments in the company by which I was employed.

Many years ago I formed a personal holding company into which I placed a large part of my investment holdings, in exchange for its entire stock. The company was called the Broseco Corporation. Subsequently, there having been created outstanding preferred stock of this company, I conveyed the preferred stock to my children, then still minors, as gifts to be held by them severally in trust pending the reaching of a stipulated age in each case. These gifts were made after the gift-tax laws had been enacted, but prior to the time it was made known that the gift taxes would be increased.

For many years I looked forward to the day when I would be in a position to devote time and attention to convert this company into a family enterprise, in which the stockholders, present and future, could find the satisfaction which comes from playing a part, small though it might be, in the productive field of industry, and contributing thereby to the constructive course of our national economy.

Upon retirement in 1946, I began to give thought to these long-felt aspirations, and gradually turned toward opportunities in the petroleum industry. It happened that soon after retirement, I was invited by the Mellon interests to consider going on the Board of the Gulf Oil Corporation. After going into the matter thoroughly, I accepted the proposal, which led to a surrender of a substantial amount of GM stock in exchange for Gulf stock. During the succeeding 10 years, as a member of the Board, I served as a member of its Finance Committee, its Executive Committee, and for most of the time as Chairman of its Incentive Compensation Plan Committee. The problems of the industry were deeply interesting, and the personal associations with directors and executives of the Corporation were most pleasant and gratifying.

In this way I became familiar with the economic phases of the oil industry, and came to see that the field of oil or gas exploration offered favorable opportunities for my personal holding company to achieve the objectives I had in view. I discussed the matter with my Gulf associates, who saw no objection to my personal activities in this area, provided, of course, that due care be taken to avoid any possibility of conflict of interest as between myself personally and the Gulf Oil Corporation.

Following some efforts along this line, which did not

prove fruitful in any substantial sense, I came into contact in 1953 with a small, independent oil operator in Texas, Neville G. Penrose. After several discussions, we decided there were real opportunities in an arrangement whereby the Broseco Corporation would acquire a one-third interest in the Penrose operations. This would make possible something in the nature of a partnership relationship with his organization in the oil business. I explored this idea with the Gulf people, and again they imposed no objections, with the continued understanding that there be no conflict of interests involved so long as I remained on the Board.

The deal with Penrose was consummated, he having accepted the restriction upon his activities made necessary by my Gulf connection. Broseco had no personnel in its direct organization competent as operators in the oil business, and I had no idea of it creating an operating organization within itself. The intention was, and continues to be, that the Penrose organization function in the manner of an "oil department" of Broseco, serving the mutual interests of the parties dependent upon it. The relationship through the years between Broseco and the Penrose organization has been pleasing in every way, and considerable progress has been made in fulfilling the objectives I had. In fact, by reason of its oil activities, Broseco has come into the status of an operating company, removed from that of a "personal holding company" and the limitations which are imposed by law upon that type of organization.

Around the middle of 1956, because of the progress which had been achieved in association with Penrose, I decided it was not fair to him to continue the restriction imposed by my membership on the Gulf Board. I went into the situation with my Gulf associates, and it was mutually agreed that in the circumstances I should retire. They urged that I give up the other connection, or continue to maintain the restrictions which had existed; but the die was cast, and I was unwilling to do so. So, I retired in July, 1956. My resignation was accepted with expressions of genuine regret, and I received messages in the same vein from my companions in Gulf of 10 years standing. These have been deeply gratifying.

Thinking about the future, and reminiscing about the past, I am reminded once more how the one is, inevitably, an extension of the other, and how each event in life, big or little, helps to shape tomorrow's destinies. This is the procession of history, but it finds its most intimate and meaningful expression in the immediate family. Mrs. Brown and I have six children: H. Barksdale Brown, in Pittsburgh; Frank D. Brown, Jr., in Port Deposit; Bruce F. Brown, in Detroit; Mrs. Greta B. Layton, in Wilmington; Vaughan W. Brown, in Baltimore, and Keene C. Brown, now living in New York. Through the gifts to them, mentioned above, they are in comfortable financial circumstances, which actually is a source of some embarrassment to them; each has an inner determination to make his and her own way in life through personal contributions to society. All are happily married except Keene, who is still recovering from physical handicaps suffered in a terrible automobile accident 10 years ago. At this writing, we have 16 grandchildren, but we are reasonably confident that before this narrative is read in book form, the number will be 17. So make it 16½ grandchildren; the fractional contribution referring to the expectations of Vaughan and his wife, who were married in the summer of 1956! All of the children and grandchildren are a happiness and comfort to the aging parents.

Broseco Corporation stands in my mind as representing in a sense a family enterprise, and it is my hope that our children, when coming into possession of the residue of our estates, will regard it as such, even though it may not provide direct employment for them. Barksdale, the oldest, has been in Gulf's employment for some years, and carrying on, I'm told, very creditably, looking upon that occupation as his future life-time career. He is ruled out, therefore, from taking any direct place in the affairs of Broseco. Frank owns the farm and dairy operation which was once in my possession, is deeply interested in that and in active service in various civic affairs of the community. Bruce is happily employed with General Motors in Detroit. Greta's husband is a member of a well-known law firm in Wilmington, and unlikely to be diverted from the practice of law. Vaughan has other ideas in mind, and Keene is presently limited in the scope of his activities by the physical handicaps I have mentioned. Throughout all the years that have been tragic to him, he has displayed marvelous courage, with steadfastness and determination accompanied by a high order of mental capacity, and a fine congeniality of spirit. Now living in his own apartment in New York, he has been taking special courses at Columbia University, and measuring up most creditably.

All but two of the children are members of the Board of Broseco; the two ineligible being Barksdale, because of his Gulf connections, and Bruce, because of his remoteness from headquarters. Due to the dependence which Broseco places upon the Penrose organization for actual operations, however, Broseco itself does not offer the potential to members of the family for constructive service through full-time management participation. Besides the thought and attention which I give to the affairs of Broseco, its direction is provided by John B. Rich, the active executive officer, as Vice President, who is highly competent to carry on his important duties. For many years Mr. Rich also has been handling the investment affairs of Mrs. Brown and our children, and he is named in Mrs. Brown's will and my own as co-executor and co-administrator of our estates.

I look hopefully on Broseco to continue its activity in the oil business, with of course a shrinkage in its assets which must occur when estate taxes are met. Members of the family on its Board are now concerned, and will continue to be, with the problems of basic policy inherent in such an enterprise, and I know they will play the constructive roles which will be called for. Mr. Rich will be depended upon to meet the essential needs of executive administration, with suitable thought given in preparing for the day when he, himself, will insist upon relinquishing the arduous duties now resting upon him.

Over the past years Mrs. Brown and I made annual grants to charity and other worthy causes from marginal funds available for that purpose. Often, with uncertainties existing as to the amount of income applicable, we would have to wait until near the end of the year before determining upon grants to be extended. Then we would be bothered by the difficulties of deciding, in an orderly manner, on the proper apportionments to causes deemed worthy. For these reasons, I set up a few years ago the Mt. Ararat Foundation, which carries certification of tax exempt status under Section 170 (c) of the Internal Revenue Code. Mrs. Brown and I now extend gifts annually to this Foundation giving due regard to the deductability from taxable incomes, so as to conserve basic resources in the interest of posterity. There is no intention of building up unused resources within the Foundation. But the procedure being followed allows us far better opportunity to deal with the problems of annual grants to worthy causes on an orderly and considered manner.

In this narrative I had occasion to mention a brother, the late John Thompson Brown, and several sisters. Two sisters have not been mentioned: Mrs. P. B. Adsit, living at Pleasantville, N. Y., and Mrs. Frank H. Merrill, living in Baltimore.

The former sister is Peachy, which is her real name; her great grandmother was Susanna Peachy Poythress, the wife of John Vaughan Willcox, whose home was the plantation Flower de Hundred, near Petersburg, Virginia. Following Dad's failure in 1903, Peachy entered the Nursing School of Johns Hopkins, but was diverted from that career when she fell in love with a young intern. Her husband, the late Harry Adsit, was a prominent graduate of the Johns Hopkins Medical School, and there are two fine children, both worthy citizens. I lived with Peachy and her doctor husband after starting to work in Baltimore, and always have been very close to this sister. Peachy is some years older than I, but we remain close to this day, in spite of, or perhaps because of, her inclination to display a "motherly" attitude towards me!

". . . this good wife . . . a helpmate of the highest order."

Mrs. Merrill — Eleanor Plunkett — was named after an intimate friend of ancestors in the British Isles. "Plunk," as most of us call her, became a secretary and lived with a sister and brother-in-law, the John M. Glenns, first in Baltimore and later in New York. She served in the Red Cross overseas during World War I, and afterwards joined the staff of the National Society for the Prevention of Blindness. She became Executive Director of that organization, from which position she retired some years ago. Her husband, the late Frank H. Merrill, had been a widower and was a fine person. They married somewhat late in life and had no children. "Plunk" is close to the whole family, and is affectionately called by her nickname by all of the nieces and nephews. She is my kid sister, and hence duly respectful of my superior age — no "motherly instincts" like the older sisters!

One other sister is living; Fanny, the oldest, who appears in the reminiscences about the Glencoe days of my youth (Chapter I). Fanny, who never married, has been living in a charming small house in White Plains, New York. She has artistic talents, managerial ability, and a love of people. Fanny and I enjoy frequent visits, which are marked by fierce struggles at the game of Canasta.

I could not conclude this narrative without something more about my wife, Greta, whose encouragement, sympathetic understanding and marvelous good sense have been profoundly influential in every phase of my business career. We were engaged to be married in 1913, but only her parents, Mr. and Mrs. Barksdale, were told about it. The reason for delaying our marriage was economic; as mentioned in Chapter II, I had borrowed money from her father, and was unwilling to marry until all my debts were paid off, and I could see my way clear to support a family. Greta accepted this viewpoint sympathetically, as did her parents. When security for the future was assured, and I felt confident of my ability to meet the responsibilities, public announcement of our engagement was made, and we were married in June, 1916.

Over all the years this good wife of mine has been a helpmate of the highest order. On all fundamental concepts we have seen eye to eye, not only with regard to the raising of our children, but also on those difficult problems arising from my business activities which sometimes caused me great anguish and uncertainty. It must not be assumed that the progress of my career was free from severe setbacks, differences of opinion with business associates, and other serious and painful experiences. On the contrary, it was inevitable that such agonizing times should occur. There were times when it seemed to me that I had been deserted by my closest friends; others, when I was tempted to doubt the value and the wisdom of my own decisions on critical issues. At such times, my wife always was a source of renewed courage and faith, strengthening me with sympathy and encouragement.

Of course we have experienced closely together all of the joys and the heartaches which intermingle for parents in the raising of a family. Above all, she has helped to keep my feet on the ground, overcoming with tact and patience and enormous comprehension the hazards which have come to me from personal idiocyncracies.

THE END

APPENDIX

A LETTER FROM A FATHER TO HIS SONS

Petersburg, Virginia
1833

My dear Sons:

As life is uncertain and I may not live until you reach the age of discretion, I have determined to commit to paper, for your benefit in the event of my death, a few facts and sentiments which it seems to me important that you should know and have impressed upon your minds. At present I write in much haste, without leisure and reflection which are necessary to make the result satisfactory to myself and with an intention, at the first convenient opportunity, of revising and rewriting this somewhat imperfect sketch. Should such an opportunity never be offered, it will still be some satisfaction to have left even this crude memorial, which, as it is designed only for your private and personal use, will not be exposed to public view or unfriendly criticism.

You will naturally have some curiosity on the subject of your ancestors, and as such matters rest chiefly in tradition and may otherwise be lost to you, I will give you the fruits of my inquiries. I have a two-fold object in doing so, as it will satisfy you that the humility of your origin leaves no ground for (that most weak and contemptible of all feelings under a republican government) aristocratic pretensions, whilst the unsullied respectability of the whole family, paternal and maternal, as far as my knowledge extends, will give you a just confidence and commendable pleasure in the only point which should awaken any solicitude, the honesty of your ancestry.

The tradition of my family is that our ancestors, John and Henry Brown, came to Virginia at an early period under the auspices of their kinsman Sir William Brown, one of the original Virginia Company, and that they were of some influence and distinction, which is rendered more probable by the recurrence of such names (perhaps slightly altered by the incorrect orthography of the times) in the ancient statutes of the State, for instance in the 1st volume of Hening's Statutes at Large, pages 138, 235, 282, 288, 322, 339, 517 et passim.

There are no further certain accounts of the family until the year 1755 when Henry Brown, my great-grandfather, was living on his farm in what is now Botetourt, then Augusta County, on the bank of the Roanoke River a few miles from Salem, a spot which I have since visited. He had then two sons by his first marriage, Henry, my grandfather, and Samuel, the father of the late Col. Samuel Brown of Greenbrier, whose brother, Adam, was captured by a party of Indians at an early age and spent his life amongst them near Detroit, a place called Brownstown. My great-grandfather, by his second marriage, had sons, Thomas, Robert and a daughter, Esther Carlton. My grandfather was then a widower, having three daughters, one of whom named Ann afterwards married a Mr. Adams.

An event occurred this year (1755) in the Fall, after Braddock's defeat, which made it a memorable era in the history of the family. The residence of my great grandfather was on the then frontiers of the state and exposed to the frequent incursions of the Indians. It was customary to keep fire arms loaded and in perfect readiness, so that the family might be said to sleep on their arms. My grandfather had placed his infant children farther down in the settlements for security, while he remained with his father on the Roanoke. His brother, Samuel, had removed to Greenbrier and his half brother, Thomas, was absent in the militia service. My grandfather observed early in the morning some moccasin tracks and, suspecting they were Indians, came home and informed his father of it. They were sitting in the house examining their guns when a party of five Indians, supposed to be Shawnees, fired in upon them through the door and windows and instantly killed the old man and his wife. Henry, my grandfather, shot the chief dead as he entered the door and then, springing out with his gun clubbed, he attacked another Indian who was pressing forward. A long doubtful struggle ensued. Robert, who was in view, said my grandfather laid his blows about him manfully. At one time he was brought on his knees by a stroke from the breech of the Indian's gun, which left a large knot on his forehead which was visible until his death. Robert, meanwhile, fired from the interior of the house and wounded another Indian. The remaining two Indians, who were disengaged and preparing for scalps and plunder, finding their leader fallen, another wounded, a third well matched and probably fearing there were more men in the house from which Robert had fired, picked up the wounded man and retreated towards the river. Just at this moment my grandfather had succeeded in giving his antagonist a severe blow in the face, upon which he yelled aloud and followed his comrades. My grandfather then scalped the chief, took his rifle and ornaments and went to a fort four miles below with his clothes torn, bloody and covered with paint. Having procured assistance, he returned and buried the dead. He then went to Williamsburg, carrying the gun and ornaments of the Indian Chief and received the large reward (£30 or perhaps £50) offered by the laws of the state for the scalp of an Indian killed by a private citizen. Governor Dinwiddie offered him a commission in the army, which he declined in consequence of the exposed situation of his family and property.

He now bought a farm in Bedford County, on Otter Creek, where he resided during the balance of his life and on which my father still resides. He built him a large stone house, which was in a state of tolerable preservation at the period of my earliest recollections and the ruins of which may still be seen. It was long and low with small windows and massy walls, resembling more a fort than a modern mansion, a style of building probably suggested by apprehensions growing out of a vivid remembrance of the disastrous fate of his family and the still dangerous vicinity of the Indians.

He shortly afterwards married Alice Bard of N. Carolina, of whose family I know nothing except that it was of Irish extraction and from Belfast. He had by her three sons, Henry (my father), Samuel and Daniel and some daughters. Samuel was educated with some care and became a Presbyterian clergyman. He was a man of great learning and ability—resided in Rockbridge County, much loved and respected by his congregation, and died in 1822. A neat tombstone in the graveyard of the church near Brownsburg evinces the esteem and regret of his neighbors. Daniel grew wealthy by mercantile pursuits and died at his residence in Lynchburg in 1821. My father inherited the homestead, upon which he has resided all his life in a rural and retired manner. His estate was increased by a mercantile connection with his brother Daniel and James Leftwich, of whom he was a dormant partner.

In his youth he was active and adventurous, so much so that his education was greatly neglected, as may be inferred from the circumstances of his quitting school to join a hunting party going to Kentucky to kill buffaloes. He was at the battle of Guilford in N. Carolina in 1781 as a volunteer in a company of riflemen raised in this county and commanded by Capt. Moon, his friend and neighbor, in Lynch's corps, of the Virginia line of militia in Green's army. He met the attack of Cornwallis after the N. Carolina line had fled, and was wounded early in the action by a musket ball in the thigh, passing through the hip. As soon as he fell, he was carried off the field by two men, named Fitzhugh and Bargamin, to a mill 3 miles distant, where he found his Captain wounded and dying. On the next day he was carried up to the main army at Speedwell's iron works, eight miles from the battle ground, and thence to the Hospital on Dan River. He was taken home by his father from the latter place on a litter, and was confined with his wound for several years. In 1795 he married Frances Thompson, the daughter of John Thompson, who had served in the Virginia line with credit throughout the revolutionary war and died where he was born, in Campbell County, near New London, after a long life devoted to agriculture.

My father has been remarkable throughout his life for his quiet and unambitious deportment—for the kindness and benevolence of his disposition and the surpassing excellence of his judgment. He was for many years of pious habits but never attached himself to a church until the year 1831 when he joined the Baptists and was publicly baptized notwithstanding his advanced age. He was as liberal, indulgent and affectionate a father as any man ever had, and under a negligent exterior and careless style of expression (adhering scrupulously to the ancient uses and pronunciation of words) he displayed to all who knew him well a mind of the very highest order and a heart replete with every good and generous quality. My mother is remembered by the family chiefly for her personal beauty—her piety and uncommon affection for her children.

With the history of your maternal kindred I am not so well acquainted but can give you some general outlines. Your grandfather, John Vaughan Willcox, is descended from a family of English extraction; his father was a highly respectable merchant of Charles City county; and one of his remote ancestors of the same name appears to have been a lawyer and legislator as early as 1623, as may be seen from 1st volume of Hening's Statutes at Large, pages 129, 414, 421, 431. Your grandmother, whose maiden name was Susanna Peachy Poythress, is represented by all her acquaintances to have been the most excellent and interesting of women. Her ancestors, for many generations, resided at their family seat on James River, called Flower de Hundred, which once belonged to the Governor, Sir George Yeardley. One of her ancestors, Francis Poythress, of whom some notice is taken in Hening's Statutes at Large, pages 289, 318, 353, 359, was a county lieutenant and commanded the forces of the colony in an expedition in 1645 against Opechancanough, King of the Pamunkeys and brother of Powhattan. He was instructed to build a fort in the Rappahanock unless he should succeed in subduing, or negotiating with, the Indians. The county of Northumberland in the conquered country was shortly afterwards established, and he represented it in the Assembly as a burgess.

Your mother, I trust, will long live to give you a happy demonstration of her admirable character and exalted virtues, and I need only add that, when you know her, you cannot fail to discover in her, in a greater degree than in any other woman I have ever known, all those rare and noble qualities which will compel you to honour and love her as a mother.

I shall not indulge in the egotism of saying much of myself, as you can learn all that you may desire to know from my contemporaries. I graduated at Princeton, sharing the first honors of a large class with James Bayard of Pennsylvania and Wm. Peronneau Finley of Charleston, S. Carolina, the latter of whom was throughout my college career, and has been ever since, the most intimate friend I have ever had, excepting my parents and my brother Henry. I studied law with Chancellor Creed Taylor and commenced the practice of my profession in Harrison County, which I have the honor shortly afterward to represent in the General Assembly.

I have said this much of your ancestry in order to show you that, whilst you have nothing to boast of on that score, you have nothing to regret or be ashamed of; and I fervently pray that you may so fill up the measure of your days as not to detract from, if you do not add to, this stock of honest reputation.

As the course of your education in the event of my death is a subject of much concern to me, I have appointed guardians for you in my will. I have directed that the older brother shall be educated if possible at the Military Academy at West Point and that the younger shall be bred in the Navy. I have seen much of the world myself and have bestowed the deepest reflection on the subject of your education, and such is the result of my opinions.

I do not hold in much estimation the effects of a course of collegiate instruction and residence. Withdrawn from the world and pent up for years within college walls, the individual loses all knowledge of the busy, bustling multitude without, upon whom he must be eventually dependent and in the midst of whom the whole drama of life is to be acted. Sedentary habits enervate his body and, by sympathy, give a morbid sentimental turn to his mind. When he leaves the warm precincts of Alma Mater and comes into the world, it is not an easy transition from preparation to action, but a sudden and startling plunge into an uncongenial element. Conscious of his own superior learning, he looks with a certain feeling of contempt on the crowd of his fellow creatures, whom he regards as his inferiors in all respects. Instead of viewing knowledge as a mere weapon which to be useful must be wielded with boldness and dexterity, he thinks it a kind of talisman which, of itself, is to bring the favors of fortune into his lap without an effort on his part. Crammed with abstract principles and pure science but incapable from want of discipline of wielding them with ease and effect, the inert mass seems merely to paralyze his mind, as a soldier is crushed under the weight of a too heavy armour. Too proud to go down into the arena and contend for the palm amidst dust and sweat, ignorant of human nature, unacquainted with business, undervaluing all that is not specious and refined, learned but destitute of common sense, he is of all description of persons the least prepared to adapt himself to the habits which are indispensable to success in any of those pursuits to which in this country all are destined; and is uniformly exposed to the mortification of seeing himself outstripped by men of far less genius, knowledge and refinement, but of far more of those homely but necessary qualities and acquirements which are so extensively engaged in carrying on the various operations of the social machine.

Do not understand me as depreciating the advantages of education. On the contrary, I look with a degree of veneration and even affection on all the institutions which are calculated to enlarge and exalt the human mind. (I wish you, my sons, previous to going into the army and navy, which will not be until your fourteenth or fifteenth years, to devote yourselves diligently to the study of the ancient languages and the classics, so as to lay the ground work of extensive learning and good taste. At my fifteenth year, I had gone through the usual course of reading in the Latin and Greek languages.) But my opinion is that knowledge is of little value unless you can command it at any moment and that this facility can only be acquired by uniting practice with study. In travelling through this insolent world of ours I would rather carry a pistol in my pocket than a blunderbuss at the bottom of my trunk.

Knowledge, moreover, is of no value unless accompanied with good health, which can only be preserved by exercising the physical equally with the mental faculties. That education then is the best which gives the greatest expansion to the bodily as well as the intellectual powers, which unites the practical with the profound— and leads the individual by an easy transition from the labors of the closet to the stage of action. The course of studies at the Military Academy is admirably calculated to give strength and scope to the mind, whilst the military part of the discipline insures the sound and healthful state of the body. In the Navy the system of instruction, though different, is perhaps equally beneficial, leading to personal hardihood, foreign travel, with abundant leisure for study on board ship, and all this in the course of a reputable discharge of a public duty to the country.

Should you both spend your early years in laying the foundation of a capacious store of knowledge, remain in the army and navy until you attain the ranks of lieutenants, then return to private life with an intention of resuming the service whenever your country calls you to the field. I can hardly doubt that you will be all that my fondest solicitude could wish you to be. Instead of being merely soldiers and sailors "full of strange oaths and bearded like the pard," I anticipate that you will be intelligent, discreet and virtuous, showing by your walk and manner that you are "every inch of you a man"—bold, manly and independent, acquainted with human nature—of practical good sense— of a refinement of manner and sentiments resulting from the consciousness of truth and honor, taking your place among your fellow creatures, as if you were one of them, without an effort, like a rational member of the human family, ready for the various duties that may devolve on you. Should such be the effect of your education and such your character on returning to society, I may safely leave it to you to select for yourselves your future pursuits or employment.

Allow me, however, to add a few precepts which may be applicable to all conceivable situations in which you can be placed. Impress it on your thoughts, from early life, that you are created for noble purposes, accustom yourself to believe that there is no human dignity or grandeur to which you may not aspire rationally, provided you employ the necessary means. The greatest men who have ever lived were of lowly birth, without a tithe of the advantages you will enjoy. But mark it, my sons, they were men of temperance, industry, frugality and of lofty but virtuous and patriotic ambition. They learned while their nature was yet pliant to make their *passions* subordinate to *reason,* and instead of wasting their youth in indolence or frivolous pleasure, they began at once in the vigor and freshness of the morning, while the day was yet before them, to climb the steep and rugged hill of fame. He who hopes to reach the summit must begin betimes or old age will arrest him in the midst of his progress. It is in youth that the fatal error of life is generally committed. Genius feels conscious of its powers and resolves to spend the spring time of existence in ease and pleasure or else, elated with some partial triumphs, sleeps on its laurels until, when again at length aroused to assert its supremacy, its edge is blunted and its energies destroyed by inaction—the favored season of exertion is passed, the future then is too short to consummate a plan of life, and the proud spirit sinks under the accumulated weight of remorse and despair. If then you wish to win for yourselves a name that may be honored by your friends and your country, begin betimes I charge you; or if you prefer to fill up the measure of your usefulness in the noiseless and unambitious discharge of the duties which belong to private life, and which are not the less important because they are minute and various, again I say, begin betimes. And whatever your aim or your condition, bear these considerations in mind, my sons, and let them be the landmarks of your conduct.

You are now blessed with a spotless character, a reputable ancestry, and under the whole canopy of heaven have in right and in trust no superior. Preserve your name and character through life, as pure and virtuous as it now is. Be plain, uniform and unassuming in your manners, habits and dress. Learn to respect the manly good sense which always resides in the mass of the people—cherish a habitual sentiment of benevolence for mankind, of patriotism for your country, and of reverence for your Creator, through faith in the Christian religion. Assume a lofty and manly mode of thinking and acting—affect supcriority over no one and acknowledge no superior—let your outward manners be modest and gentle, but let your heart be fearless and resolute. Be just and fear not. Meet your fellowman in all the transactions of life, face to face—do justice to him and compel him to do justice to you. Never for an instant, nor for the sake of temporary advantages, swerve in the least from the direct line of honor and integrity. Do nothing which will lessen you in your own esteem, for your own consciousness of your own rectitude is of far more importance to you than the approbation of the world.

These are rigid precepts but they are founded in wisdom and virtue, and without the observance of them you never can be happy. Let no consideration tempt you to violate them. Let no fear of consequences deter you—no hope of temporary advantage allure you—from the faithful discharge of your duties. This course may at times bring you into trouble. The good and the great are not always fortunate. You may be poor—persecuted—afflicted—but never regard that. Under the worst extremities of fortune, you will have what will cheer and sustain you through good and through evil, a conscience and a heart at peace with themselves; and what is of infinitely more consequence than all, besides you will have the animating reflections of a virtuous and well spent life, to console and recompense you in the hour of death.

Your affectionate father

John Thompson Brown

To my sons
Henry & John

Opposite page: GM monthly report form on financial results of divisional operations. (See page 48.)

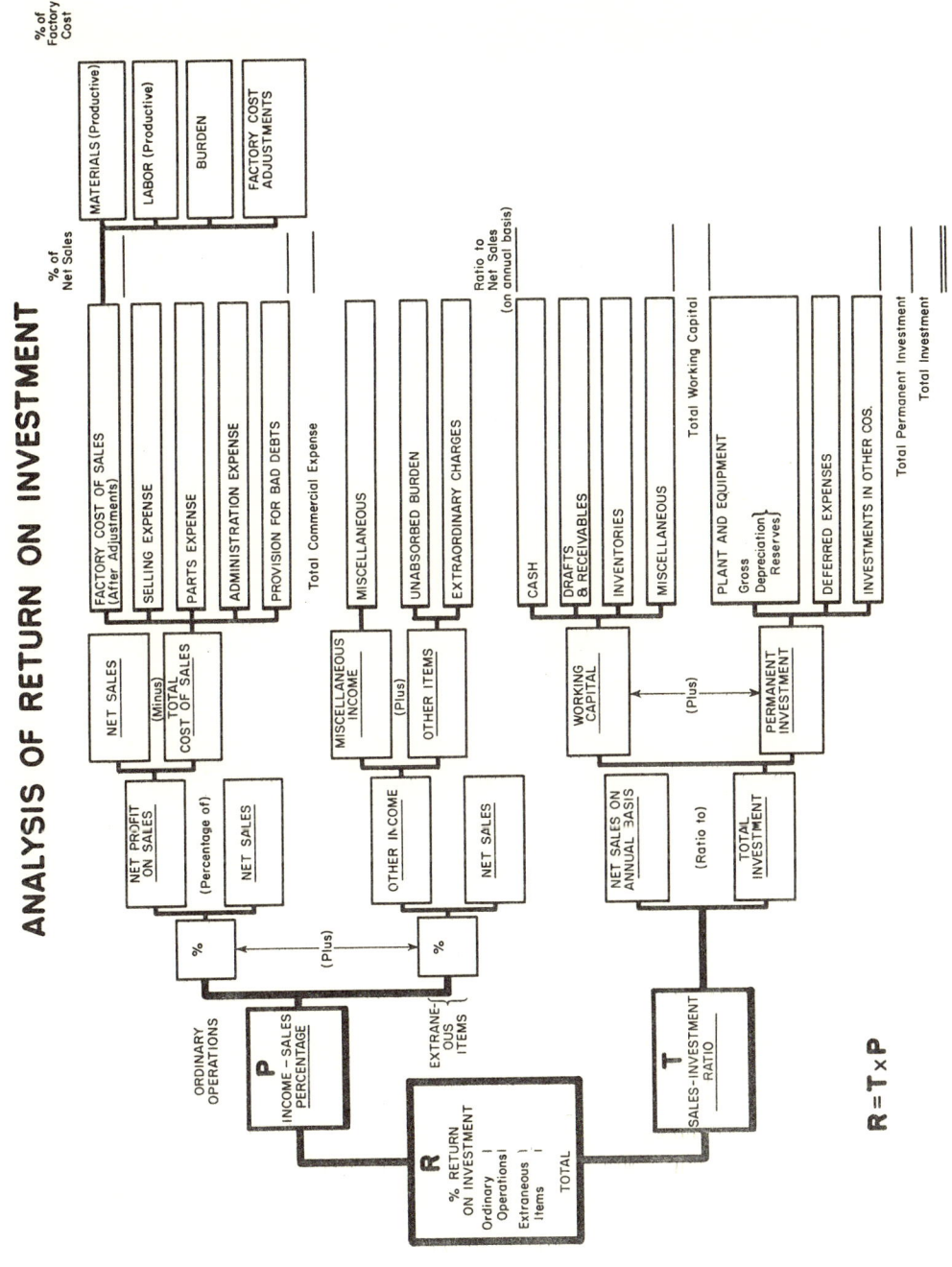

PRICING POLICY IN RELATION TO FINANCIAL CONTROL

By DONALDSON BROWN
Vice-President, General Motors Corporation

I—PRINCIPLES INVOLVED

The problem of modern industrial management holds two aspects, quite separate and distinct in basic character. On the one hand lie the governing considerations of return on investment and protection of capital employed; on the other, the correlated considerations of operating procedure and detail. In the broad sense the interests of capital are represented by a board of directors and such subcommittees as may be constituted, having jurisdiction over policies; while authority and responsibility for operating results are lodged with executive officers and subordinate departments.

Sound policies must be founded upon a knowledge of the nature and characteristics of the individual business, and the point of view of the executive in actual contact with the operating necessities and difficulties is essential. Intimacy with the daily operating problems leads to intelligent decisions of policy, and thus it is that organization often takes the form of committee management, where questions of policy are dealt with by the board of directors or a representative committee comprised of departmental executives. This form of management possesses the attribute that the departmental executive is called upon to administer policies in the formulation of which he has had a direct voice, and may be said theoretically to afford the maximum of opportunity for the co-ordination of the two aspects of management. Practically, however, it always renders more difficult the differentiation between questions of policy and operating procedure. Policies should be dealt with from an impartial understanding of the operating aspect, and in the exercise of the dual function it is difficult for the individual to divorce himself from the departmental viewpoint.

Questions of policy merge themselves with questions of operating procedure so that frequently it is difficult to dissociate the two. In a moderate-sized business where ownership and management are identical, and where the departmental executives are in actual contact with the detail operating problems, there may even be no conscious segregation of the broad questions of policy. Decisions are made for executive action which involve a composite consideration of all of the elements involved, and the interests of capital are served by direct control. In modern industry, however, where economies of manufacture and distribution are derived from large-scale operation, ownership and management cannot be identical. Capital is derived from various sources and from many stockholders identified only to a limited extent with management

The magnitude and financial strength of General Motors is such that it is enabled to effect great economy in manufacture and distribution. Its organization is designed so that these advantages may be enjoyed without the sacrifice of co-ordinate control so often experienced in big business. The corporation comprises a number of divisions which manufacture and sell passenger cars and commercial vehicles of non-competitive classes, and numerous divisions whose production of component parts and accessories is sold both to General Motors divisions and to outside automobile companies. Each division is equipped with a self-contained organization having complete jurisdiction over manufacture, sales, and finance, subject to control from the central authority. The ordinary, everyday questions of policy, embodying even such important matters as production schedules, inventory commitments, design of product, and methods of distribution, are left ordinarily within the consideration and decision of the divisions themselves, under certain general limitations, and in every way the men on the firing line are inspired with a sense of responsibility for results.

The central organization embraces talent in automotive engineering and research, and experts dealing with important problems of improved methods of manufacture and distribution, all of whom serve in a more or less advisory capacity. Apart from these important adjuncts, and certain necessary activities in finance and accounting, law, and related matters, the central organization deals almost exclusively with questions of policy. The president is general manager of the corporation in fact, but controls the operations by the establishment of principles and the interpretation of policies, and refrains from entering into questions of operating detail except in cases where the two are inseparable. The Executive and Finance Committees, as active bodies subject to the board of directors, have final jurisdiction over the entire business through the enunciation of policies and by direct action in matters involving essential points of policy.

This brief description of the character of organization is given as illustrating the fact that the management of General Motors is such as to afford a peculiarly good opportunity for segregation of the broad questions of policy which are of fundamental concern in the interests of the stockholders. One phase of the problem lies in the direction of formulating policies in such terms as to render them understandable, so that they will actually govern executive action and at the same time not hamper the exercise of initiative on the part of those responsible for operations. It is to this phase of the problem that the present discussion is directed.

One of the most important necessities of policy has to do with financial control. Expansion must be limited within the resources of capital, and in a corporation such as General Motors, the available capital must be directed into channels that hold the greatest promise. Capital must be derived from undivided profits or from the sale of securities, and the amount available from these sources must be measured in the light of its economic cost, with due regard to dividend income to which the stockholders are entitled. General Motors employs a very comprehensive scheme of forecasts of the prospective earnings and capital position of the corporation, to supply the basis of financial control.

CONTROL OF CAPITAL BY FORECAST

Space does not permit the presentation of a complete outline of the forecast scheme. A brief description is necessary, however, since it is through this that the Finance and Executive Committees are kept informed and thus enabled to exercise such control as may be needed from time to time.

In December of every year, each division is required to present an outline of its view of probable operations for the succeeding year, embodying estimates of sales, earnings, and capital requirements. These outlines are in three forms, i. e.: "pessimistic," representing a minimum expectation; "conservative," representing what is considered a likely condition, and "optimistic," representing what the name implies, with production and sales capacity as a limitation.

Obviously in a business such as the automobile business it is not possible to forecast conditions accurately so far as twelve months ahead, and these annual compilations are not accepted as a basis of commitments, but, with due allowance for elements of error, they are of valuable assistance in guiding the general plans and policies of the corporation.

Definite forecasts are submitted monthly, on the twenty-fifth of each month, by each division, covering the current month and the succeeding three months. These forecasts cover sales and production each month, and indicate the amount of investment at the end of each month in plant, and working capital items, and also outstanding inventory commitments. If these forecasts are accepted they constitute authority for each division, respectively, to proceed upon the manufacturing schedule and to make forward commitments for materials up to the requirements of the forecast, in the judgment of the division manager. Special authority is required from the central office to cover any commitment beyond the requirements of these authenticated forecasts.

FORECASTING AND PRICE POLICY

All forecasts, as submitted, are scrutinized by the central office and compared with current and past performance, attention of the proper officials being called to any abnormalities or marked deviations from what might be deemed a conservative sales expectation. Experience has led to the establishment of standards of working capital requirements in relation to volume of business and the forecasted investment in receivables and inventory is carefully checked against such standards, allowance being made for seasonal fluctuations. The tendencies of manufacturing costs and of selling and administrative expenses are observed, and profits are analyzed, with reference to the pricing policy laid down as governing the operations of a given division.

It has already been said that the forecasts supply the basis of financial control. The forecast, representing the deliberate plan of the corporation as applied to a division, must be based upon an accepted price policy since the factor of sales expectation is necessarily dependent upon the question of price. If the division manager preparing his forecast is in full understanding of the corporation's price policy, he can proceed intelligently. If not, he lacks the price requisite for formulating his expectation of sales volume. Therefore at the heart of the problem of financial control is the question of price; in fact, the whole is inevitably so interwoven that a comprehensive pricing policy must be an embodiment of a financial policy.

The question of price is one necessarily involving a great variety of considerations. While a specific price as applied to a particular product at a given time may be symbolic, it can never serve sufficiently as an expression of policy. Borrowing a definition of Webster's, there must be a manifestation of the "principles on which any measure or course of action is based, having regard to both the ends aimed at and the measures used to arrive at them." Conditions are changing continually, and there must be a common understanding of the principles embodying the corporation's policy if the organization is to be alive to any need which may arise for reconsideration of price.

To gain a price policy that is comprehensive and understandable *as a policy,* and not misunderstood as a dictation of *specific price,* requires a method founded upon acceptable theory. The following is a description of a method of price analysis that has been found to be adaptable to the situation of General Motors.

THE PRICE THEORY

It is generally accepted that the lower the price of a useful article the greater will be the demand for it. A new industry, with a product which proves to be of stable character, passes through a development period characterized by a deficiency in available supply as compared with the latent possibilities of demand. This deficiency results from limitations upon productive and distributive capacity imposed by the adjudged capital hazard, the limitations of personnel experienced in production and distribution, and the time which must elapse before additional facilities can be provided.

So long as there is a deficiency of supply the natural tendency toward an equilibrium between supply and demand will manifest itself by means of price, and the possible scope of demand will not be satisfied until the facilities of production and distribution and the ability of the industry to expand in step with a continued normal growth of demand have reached a state of balance, the point of stabilization.

Profit is, of course, a component of price. During the period of development the excess over the ultimate economic price will be reflected partly in excess costs, because of insufficient knowledge of the art of production and distribution, coupled with scarcity of experienced personnel; and partly in the profit margin, because the final balancing between supply and demand must manifest itself at that point.

Presuming a physical condition under which the supply of a commodity is augmentable, any addition to existing producing or distributing facilities requiring extra capital is dependent upon an attainable profit adjudged to be commensurate with hazard and cost of capital required.

An acceptable theory of pricing must be to gain over a protracted period of time a margin of profit which represents the highest attainable return commensurate with capital turnover and the enjoyment of wholesale expansion, with adequate regard to the economic consequences of fluctuating volume. Thus *the profit margin, translated into its salient characteristic, rate of return on capital employed, is the logical yardstick by which to gauge the price of a commodity with regard to collateral circumstances affecting supply and demand.*

The considerations which follow are consistent with this theory, and although resting upon a theoretical basis this method of price analysis is wholly practical.

Cost of Capital Fundamental Factor

Supply of a manufactured product is limited on the one hand by the peculiar difficulties in the way of enlarged production and distribution, such as scarcity of raw material or labor, lack of diffused knowledge of the art, restriction by patent rights or secret processes, etc. These limitations will reflect themselves in price of the product through costs or profit (or both) to an extent depending upon the degree of limitation. On the other hand, supply is limited by capital requirement. The method here advocated associates these limitations upon two sides of an equation and recognizes the limitations upon the capital side as fundamental.

If unlimited fresh capital could be had at a fixed interest cost, the pricing theory would be to set the price at that point which would yield the highest attainable volume so long as it be assured that each succeeding increment of volume resulting from price influence, affords added profits in excess of the interest cost of the added capital requirement. Stated another way, if at a given price and volume the profit margin is such as to yield a high rate of return on the capital employed, and if volume is susceptible of increase by price reduction, then a price reduction is desirable, provided the added volume affords an increase in aggregate profit in excess of the economic cost of the additional capital requirement.

A monopolistic industry, or an individual business under peculiar circumstances, might maintain high prices and enjoy a limited volume with very high rate of return on capital, indefinitely, at the sacrifice of wholesale expansion. Reduction of price might broaden the scope of demand, and afford an enlargement of volume highly beneficial, even though the rate of return on capital might be lower. The limiting considerations are the economic cost of capital, the ability to increase supply, and the extent to which demand will be stimulated by price reduction.

Thus it is apparent that the object of management is not necessarily the highest attainable *rate of return* on capital, but rather the highest return consistent with attainable volume, care being exercised to assure profit with each increment of volume that will at least equal the economic cost of additional capital required. Therefore the fundamental consideration is the economic cost of capital to the individual business.

As a matter of fact there is never an unlimited supply of capital at a fixed interest cost, and the economic cost of capital embraces the questions of capital position, availability of capital within the business to meet the requirements of added volume, sources of additional capital, and the position of the common stockholders or proprietors as affected by their contribution of an appropriate part of the capital employed, through retention of earnings or otherwise.

NEED OF A BASIC PRICING POLICY

In the absence of a governing policy, the pricing of product is likely to be haphazard and inconsistent with the primary considerations. In any event the complexity of the problem is apparent, the elements involved, while not all susceptible of exact analysis, being present in fact. Unless those elements are considered in orderly form they are more than likely to lose their relative significance.

Therefore there is always the need of a basic pricing policy that is sufficiently definite and inclusive to afford effective control, with its constituents sufficiently separable to facilitate continued scrutiny, so that necessity for modification will be detected promptly. As serving these essentials, a sound pricing policy must be founded upon a clear conception of what might be implied in the phrase *economic return attainable upon the capital required.*

BEARING OF AVERAGE CAPITAL TURNOVER

The average capital turnover of a manufacturing business, apart from other considerations, varies according to the degree of fluctuation in volume, which condition is intensified by high proportionate fixed investment. Facilities must be maintained to take care of peak volume, and the farther the peak is removed from the average volume the lower the average productivity of fixed facilities. With equivalent average costs and price of product the average return on capital employed in the case of one plant operating at an average of 85 per cent of capacity will be greater than in the case of an equivalent plant operating at an average of 75 per cent of capacity. Either the capacity of plant must be greater or the average volume less in the latter case, and the productivity of the capital correspondingly less.

In the case of two competing establishments situated respectively as just cited the relative return attainable upon capital will be affected directly by the conditions named. Furthermore, so long as the return is greater than the economic cost of capital, and demand may be increased by price reduction, the rate of return that is desirable to govern the pricing of product is qualified by the question of capital turnover, even where there is no competition or where the rate of capital turnover is common throughout a competitive industry. This is because at a given rate of return on capital the percentage profit margin is indirectly proportionate to the rate of capital turnover, and a wide margin supplies a corresponding latitude for stimulation of demand.

In other words, a reduction of 5 per cent in price might have an equivalent stimulation upon demand, but due to its proportion of the profit margin, the resultant volume might in one case afford added profit in excess of the economic cost of additional capital requirement, while in another case of higher capital turnover the added volume might afford no added profit, or that which is less than the economic cost of the additional capital requirement.

The rate of return attainable upon capital is interlocked with the question of capital turnover, and a measure of the normal average capital turnover is necessary in forming a conception of the economic return attainable.

Pricing Policy Must Consider Average Return

While it is ordinarily recognized that return on investment is the basis of a pricing policy, the usual procedure lacks the complement of a systematic gauge as to the suitable variation of return in periods of relatively high or low volume. Capital is not attracted, except for speculative purposes, by a temporary opportunity for return, but by the promise of a suitable ultimate average, coupled with the element of amortization where permanency is not assured. With this attribute recognized, it becomes obviously confusing to treat with the pricing question upon a plane of capital return in specific periods when, by the nature of things, the basis must be changing continually through the influence of fluctuating volume.

The adaptation of the basic pricing policy is much more orderly if it is conceived and laid down as a standard representing the average condition, and so arranging its employment for price-fixing purposes that a suitable variation in return on capital in transitory periods is automatic. Therefore economic return attainable, as used in this article, is the accepted standard which represents expectation on the basis of an ultimate average condition. It should be under continual observation and should be modified to accord with changes in fundamental conditions, but it does not vary by reason of fluctuations in volume of business.

NORMAL AVERAGE RATE OF PLANT OPERATION

The normal condition of any business of a stable character affords continued growth in step with the growth and increase of purchasing power of the community served, coupled with the broadening influences upon the scope of consumption arising from lowered prices and enlarged appreciation of the utility of the commodity. Such growth cannot follow a straight line curve, but is interrupted by conditions existing in boom periods and periods of depression. If the trend line could be exactly located it would represent a normal average condition, but quantitatively it is undergoing continual change, and possibly will at no time coincide with actual volume over any considerable period.

On the other hand, a fluctuating volume, at times above and at times below the trend line, may be normal at all times over a series of years, for volume may be said to be normal if it is suitable in view of collateral circumstances. Thus an effort to establish a definite quantity volume as normal would be meaningless except as of a given moment. Still the normal average rate of plant operation is an essential in determining average capital turnover, so it is necessary to establish a factor of some kind that is representative of a normal average condition.

If for a moment it be conceived possible to determine the average volume trend line of a business projected forward, and to predetermine the degree of fluctuation above and below the average in the course of a business cycle, it would follow that plant capacities would be maintained on the basis of average demand, with an allowable margin to take care of the excess in boom periods. Plants would operate at the point of practical capacity in years of highest volume, because the demand in such periods would be recognized as peak requirements not calling for additional capacity margin. Any capacity in excess of the requirements of the highest volume year would admittedly represent unnecessary investment upon which no return could be enjoyed. The truth of the assertion is not destroyed by the fact that conditions surrounding business are not such as to admit the exact premise as a practical matter. Capital invested in plant, if proved unnecessary, is admittedly non-productive. If the condition arises by reason of business uncertainties, and is warranted on the score of prudent management, the non-productive investment assumes the character of normal capital requirement. If it arises from the lack of reasonable analysis and judgment of business conditions it should be eliminated, in effect, from the capital upon which a pricing consideration is based. Any other course lacks justification.

Bearing of Increased Plant Capacity

The enunciation of a basic policy to govern questions of plant extension greatly furthers the orderly control of fixed investment. If this is definitely tied into the pricing policy the result is a systematic coordination between fundamental considerations that are inevitably interwoven.

To illustrate, suppose that a basic policy has been established to the effect that plant capacities, on the basis of practical annual output, shall be maintained at 125 per cent of the *judged average trend volume,* (the margin being deliberately preserved to take care of peak requirements). Then the accepted normal average rate of operation is instantly fixed at 80 per cent of the practical annual capacity. If a given plant operates at an actual average rate below 80 per cent then there is excess investment in capacity pronounced unnecessary by the terms of the established policy.

Establishment of Standard Volume

It will be found from a description of the method which follows, that the establishment of a percentage representing an assumed normal average rate of plant operation is an essential factor in the analysis of price. This determines the so-called *standard volume* which is accepted as the basis upon which costs will be measured, and upon which the margin of profit is determined as necessary to afford a given average rate of return upon capital employed. The established percentage must reflect the unavoidable fluctuations of business which render an even rate of production impossible, and as far as practicable should represent the economic situation of the industry, rather than any abnormal situation which might be recognized as pertaining to a given plant. For example, the operation of a given plant at a lower rate than competing plants leads to higher costs and increased margin of profit necessary for a given rate of return on fixed investment. Thus the establishment of a percentage that is below the average rate at which competitive plants actually operate tends towards inflation of prices above a proper economic level. Therefore, if excess capacity exists by reason of a previous misconception of the intrinsic position of the industry, or if an individual plant operates at subnormal rate, or suffers fluctuations of volume of greater magnitude than normal, resulting from misjudgment of competitive conditions or other cause, no warranty is supplied for modifying a percentage established as representing normal average rate of operation. In any such case a lowering of the established percentage would tend to intensify rather than to improve the condition.

On the other hand, if it be judged at any time that the reasonable expectations with respect to fluctuations of volume normal to the industry are of greater or less magnitude than admitted by the terms of the established policy, then the established percentage should be modified correspondingly.

Obviously it is not possible to predetermine the actual contour of a production curve, and the assumption as to the normal average rate of plant operation is a matter of judgment. So, also, is the question as to the *economic return attainable*. Prices might be maintained to yield 20 per cent average return on capital on the assumption of plants operating at an average of 80 per cent of practical annual capacity, and time might prove actual operation at an average of 65 per cent and the return 15 per cent. It would not follow necessarily that, had the actual operating condition been foreseen, 20 per cent return could have been attained. The two questions are necessarily associated, and the basic pricing policy should reflect reasonable allowances for unavoidable fluctuation of volume, requiring that the *economic return attainable* be stated at all times upon the basis of an accepted conception of the normal average rate, or attainable average rate of plant operation. This will be expressed as a percentage of practical annual capacity, and will be known as *standard volume*.

II—METHOD OF ANALYSIS

The foregoing has dealt with the principles involved in the price consideration. The following deals more concretely with the method of analysis designed to give reflection to these same principles.

Influence of Volume Fluctuations on Costs

Costs of production and distribution per unit of product must vary with fluctuation of volume, because of the uncontrollability of some of the expense items. Ordinarily, raw materials and productive labor may be referred to as 100 per cent variable, as the aggregate will vary with volume, and remain uniform per unit of product except for price changes. Among the uncontrollable items are such expenses as depreciation, taxes, etc., which may be referred to as 100 per cent fixed, since within limits of capacity the aggregate will not change, but, per unit of product, will vary indirectly with volume.

There will be a group of items, partially controllable, as to which there is no exact means of determining the degree of variation, and with respect to these it is practicable to approximate the condition by applying a factor of variability that will afford a reasonable allowance for variation in the aggregate due to changes in volume.

Generally speaking, within the limits of existing capacity, the influence of volume falls upon the final *unit cost* of product in the following way:

1. *Raw Materials and Productive Labor*—Generally unaffected by volume.

2. *Manufacturing Expenses*—Affected by volume in varying degree, according to the character of the various expenses involved, as for example:
   (a) *Fixed expenses* (such as depreciation, taxes, etc.), amount per unit of product affected in indirect proportion of volume.
   (b) *Partially controllable expenses* (such as light, heat, power, salaries, etc.) Amount per unit of product affected by volume according to the degree of variability. A factor of variability to be adjudged and applied to the current aggregate expense of the group, to arrive at the portion considered as 100 per cent variable. The remaining portion will be considered to be "100 per cent fixed."
   (c) *Controllable expenses* (such as inspection, handling of material, etc.). Amount per unit of product unaffected by volume.
3. *Commercial Expenses, in Distribution and Administration*— Affected by volume in varying degrees according to the character of the various expenses involved, as for example:
   (a) *Fixed Expenses* (such as main administrative salaries, rents, etc.) Amount per unit of product affected in indirect proportion to volume.
   (b) *Partially Controllable Expenses* (such as salesmen's and other salaries, traveling expenses, etc.) Amount per unit of product affected by volume according to the degree of variability. To be treated with as mentioned in section above under manufacturing expense.
   (c) *Controllable Expenses* (such as loading and shipping, commissions, etc.) Amount per unit of product unaffected by volume.

As unit costs are affected by fluctuation of volume, it is not practicable nor desirable to alter selling prices so as to maintain a uniform profit margin. The normal average of manufacturing expense, and distribution and administration expenses should be estimated. These, added to the raw material and productive labor cost, will give an applicable total cost on an estimated normal average basis. The pricing of product should be in relationship to costs on the normal average basis, arrived at in this manner.

TREATMENT OF MANUFACTURING EXPENSES

Manufacturing expenses are absorbed in factory costs through a burden account. If the burden rate is altered from month to month, so that the actual expense is absorbed at all times, the consequence is a distortion of costs and of inventory values due to the effect of fluctuating volume. The more acceptable accounting practice is to apply a standard burden rate, representing the proper absorption of burden at *standard volume*. In periods of low volume, the unabsorbed manufacturing expense is charged against profits as "unabsorbed burden," while in periods of high volume the overabsorbed manufacturing expense is credited to profits as "overabsorbed burden." In the interests of co-ordination it is important that *standard volume* for purposes of burden absorption shall coincide with *standard volume* for purposes of price analysis.

To arrive at the burden rate which is to be applied according to the foregoing purposes careful analysis must be made of the character of manufacturing expenses, with a view to determining the portion which is of non-controllable character. The various items should be allocated respectively to the three groups (*a*), (*b*), and (*c*) as set forth in the foregoing. As to groups (*a*) and (*c*) there is no difficulty in arriving at the non-controllable expense; the whole of class (*a*) is non-controllable, and class (*c*) holds no non-controllable expense. The degree of variability of class (*b*) has to be estimated in the light of operating experience, and it is important to keep a close follow-up analysis of this so that errors of assumption or of estimate may be corrected promptly.

The hypothetical case, Table 1, may illustrate the general principles of accounting procedure.

TABLE 1. ILLUSTRATES THE GENERAL PRINCIPLES OF ACCOUNTING PROCEDURE

	ACTUAL CURRENT CONDITION	PER CENT OF STANDARD VOLUME	ESTIMATED CONDITION AT STANDARD VOLUME
Production, Units	55,000	137.5	40,000
Productive Labor	$ 8,250,000	137.5	$ 6,000,000
Manufacturing Expenses:			
(*a*) Fixed Expenses	$ 2,000,000	100	$ 2,000,000
(*b*) Partially Controllable Expenses	9,325,000	122.7	7,600,000
(*c*) Controllable Expenses	550,000	137.5	400,000
Total Manufacturing Expense	$11,875,000	118.75	$10,000,000

It will be supposed that burden in this instance is being absorbed on the basis of productive labor. It is estimated that at *standard volume* the total aggregate manufacturing expense would be $10,000,000, and that the productive labor would be $6,000,000, thus giving a standard burden rate of 166-2/3 per cent. This burden rate would be applied, as a charge to factory cost, and with operations at 137.5 per cent of *standard volume* the overabsorbed burden would be $1,875,000 as follows:

```
Productive Labor at Current Production ........ $ 8,250,000
Burden Absorbed at Applied Burden Rate 166-2/3
    per cent ................................    13,750,000
Actual Manufacturing Expense ................    11,875,000
                                                 ──────────
Overabsorbed Burden .........................    $ 1,875,000
```

This amount would be credited to operations through an overabsorbed burden account. In this way the factory cost of product, as accounted for, is not affected by fluctuations in volume of production.

Treatment of Commercial Expenses

Commercial expenses are charged off from month to month against operations, and there is not involved the question of distortion to asset values in consequence of fluctuating volume, as in the case of manufacturing expenses. Therefore there is no need of any special accounting procedure such as that described in the foregoing. In the consideration of price, however, it is just as important to analyze the non-controllable character of commercial expenses, and to allow for the same on the basis of a normal average operating condition.

It is customary to allow for commercial expenses as a percentage of sales. The following hypothetical case, Table 2, may illustrate the general way in which this is given consideration.

In this case the allowance for commercial expenses would be 7 per cent of sales, that being the estimated condition at *standard volume,* representative of a normal average operating condition.

TABLE 2. ILLUSTRATES THE GENERAL WAY TO ALLOW FOR COMMERCIAL EXPENSES AS A PERCENTAGE OF SALES

	Actual Current Condition	Per Cent of Standard Volume	Estimated Condition at Standard Volume
Volume of Sales—Units	55,000	137.5	40,000
Volume of Sales—Amount	$68,750,000	137.5	$50,000,000
Commercial Expenses:			
(a) Fixed Expenses	$ 1,600,000	100	$ 1,600,000
(b) Partially Controllable Expenses	1,525,000	117.3	1,300,000
(c) Controllable Expenses	825,000	137.5	600,000
Total Commercial Expenses	$ 3,950,000	112.9	$ 3,500,000
Per Cent of Sales	5.75		7.0

Standards of Capital Requirement

The rate of capital turnover is usually the most important factor in a price consideration, since the margin of profit in relationship to this determines the rate of return upon capital. It is always important to maintain a statistical analysis of capital employed serving as an indication of normal capital requirements for a given volume of business, and at the same time as a basis upon which the effectiveness of control over the various investment items may be gauged.

Generally speaking, except that there may be seasonal fluctuations, the amount of capital tied up in working capital items should be directly proportionate to the volume of business. For example, the raw materials on hand should be in direct proportion to the manufacturing requirements, so many weeks' supply of this material, so many weeks' supply of that material, and so on, depending upon the condition and location of sources of supply, transportation conditions, etc. Work in process should be in direct proportion to the requirements of finished production, being dependent upon the length of time required for the material to pass from the raw to the finished state, and the amount of labor and other charges absorbed in the process. Finished product should be in direct

TABLE 3. STANDARD ESTABLISHED FOR FIXED INVESTMENT IN TERMS OF RATIO TO ANNUAL FACTORY COST OF PRODUCTION

Investment in Plant and other Fixed Assets	$15,000,000
Practical Annual Capacity	50,000 units
Standard Volume, Per Cent of Practical Annual Capacity	80 per cent
Standard Volume Equivalent	40,000 units
Factory Cost per Unit at Standard Volume	$1,000
Annual Factory Cost of Production at Standard Volume	$40,000,000
Ratio of Investment to Annual Factory Cost of Production	0.375

proportion to sales requirements. Accounts receivable should be in direct proportion to sales, being dependent upon terms of payment and efficiency of collections. Capital tied up in plant and other fixed assets is, of course, fixed investment, and should be considered in its relationship to factory cost of production.

TABLE 4. SIMILAR STANDARDS ESTABLISHED FOR WORKING CAPITAL REQUIREMENTS

	Normal Average Requirements		Standards of Capital Requirement	
	In Relation To	Turnover per Year	Ratio to Sales Annual Basis	Ratio to Factory Cost Annual Basis
Cash	Sales	20 times	0.050	
Drafts and Accounts Receivable	Sales	10 times	0.100	
Raw Material, and Work in Process	Factory Cost	6 times		0.16⅔
Finished Product	Factory Cost	12 times		0.08⅓
Gross Working Capital			0.150	0.250
Fixed Investment	Factory Cost			0.375
Total Investment			0.150	0.625

Standards of capital requirement should be established, representative of a normal average operating condition, in terms of their respective ratio to annual sales or annual factory cost of production according to whichever is the more direct relationship.

Table 3 illustrates the establishment of the *standard* of capital requirement for fixed investment. Similarly, standards are established for working capital requirements as illustrated in Table 4.

BASE PRICE STATED AS PERCENTAGE OF FACTORY COST

The basic pricing policy is expressed in terms of the *economic return attainable*. This must be interpreted, in terms of price, and enunciated as the *base price*.

Prices of product should change, in the absence of extraneous considerations, with changes in raw material and labor prices. The *base price* should be considered in relationship to cost on the normal average basis. Therefore, as previously stated, the total cost should be estimated on such basis by including with the actual raw material and productive labor cost an allowance for the normal average of uncontrollable or partially controllable expenses. In order to allow for freedom of action with respect to variations in raw material and labor prices, it is not desirable to establish the *base price* in terms of dollars per unit of product, but rather in terms of percentage of factory cost on the normal average basis.

Assuming *economic return attainable* of 20 per cent as the expression of policy, and employing the standards developed in the foregoing hypothetical cases, the following summary, Table 5, will illustrate the method of price analysis:

TABLE 5. SUMMARY ILLUSTRATING THE METHOD OF PRICE ANALYSIS

	STANDARDS	
	Ratio to Sales *Annual Basis*	Ratio to Factory Cost *Annual Basis*
Gross Working Capital....................	0.150	0.250
Fixed Investment.........................	....	0.375
Total Investment.........................	0.150	0.625
Economic Return Attainable—20 Per Cent......	....	....
Multiplying the Investment Ratio by this, the Necessary Net Profit Margin is Arrived at......	0.030	0.125
Standard Allowance for Commercial Expenses, 7 Per Cent...............................	0.070	....
Gross Margin Over Factory Cost.............	0.100 a	0.125 b

Selling Price, as a Ratio to Factory Cost...... $= \dfrac{1 + b}{1 - a} = \dfrac{1 + 0.125}{1 - 0.100} = 1.250$

Thus it is found that to derive a return of 20 per cent per annum on capital employed, the net selling price must be 1.25 times the factory cost. Therefore, Base Price Net to Company = 125 per cent.

If there is an average commission to dealers of 20 per cent, the list price at retail would be:

$$\text{Base Price, List,} = \frac{125.}{0.80} = 156.25 \text{ per cent}$$

Thus the *base price* is stated as a percentage of factory cost (on the normal average basis). There will be no change by reason of fluctuating volume and consequent variation in cost. With no change in the assumed *economic return attainable,* as representing the basic pricing policy, the *base price* will remain constant unless there is a change in assumed capital turnover.

BASE PRICE IN RELATIONSHIP TO ACTUAL PRICE

The *base price* represents a pronouncement of basic policy, and should be applied in continuing comparisons with actual prices. For example, with a *base price* of 125 per cent applied to a factory cost of $1000 per unit an indicated selling price of $1250 is arrived at to accord with the pronounced policy. This indicated selling price will be referred to as the *base price equivalent.* General correspondence between prices thus indicated and actual prices established from time to time demonstrates a state of co-ordination between the pronounced policy and administrative practice, and affords a verification of an expectancy of a given average rate of return upon capital employed. Lack of correspondence, however, does not necessarily constitute a deviation from policy. Production costs are likely to vary continually to a minor extent and selling prices ordinarily cannot be adjusted frequently, so that in establishing selling prices it is necessary to make allowances for estimated tendencies in production costs over a period of time within which a readjustment of selling prices would not be desirable. Moreover, this method of price analysis itself is such as to reflect the desirability at times of pricing product above the *base price equivalent* and at other times below.

It follows, therefore, that at a given time it is not necessarily desirable that the established price shall be in precise agreement with the *base price equivalent;* but it is essential to interpret a lack of agreement as to whether the causes are such as neither to constitute a deviation from policy nor to indicate an erroneous expectation of rate of return attainable on capital employed. An admitted deviation from the pronounced policy requires either a correction of the established price, or a revision of the assumed *economic return attainable.*

Modification of Base Price

Contact with actual operating conditions might point to errors of assumption as to normal average rate of plant operation, average capital requirement, and other assumptions and estimates employed in the basic pricing policy. Furthermore, the *base price* will be subject to modification from time to time as the assumed *economic return attainable* may be influenced by a composite of such considerations as the following:

1. Nature of the business, and its state in the progress of development up to what is usually called the point of stabilization.
2. Degree of difficulty in the way of the industry meeting a continued growth in demand, due to limitation of capital and other causes.
3. Productivity of capital in the industry and the influence of rate of return upon price, and the susceptibility of demand to price variation.
4. Availability and economic cost of capital in the case of the individual business.
5. Advantages over existing or latent competition in point of average capital turnover, and in production and distribution costs.
6. Peculiar circumstances having to do with satisfaction of demand and which are unrelated to capital turnover.
7. Good-will in the business.

Considerations in the Application of the Base Price

The preceding section indicated the kind of considerations which may lead to a modification of the *base price*. Apart from this, deviations of actual price from the *base price equivalent* in current periods may be justified by special considerations, of which the following are examples:

1. The necessity of meeting competitive conditions existing at any time, not admitted to be of a permanent character.
2. The necessity of making allowances for any extraordinary circumstances existing with respect to price of raw materials on hand or under contract, or other existing cost abnormalities.
3. Consideration must be given to the probable trend of raw material and labor costs, and allowance made for possible changes over an interval during which no price adjustment is desirable.
4. High prices in periods of high volume with correspondingly low prices in periods of low volume will tend to flatten the production curve, and consequently increase the productivity of capital employed.
5. Low prices are desirable in periods of reduced volume to stimulate demand; but a price cannot be fixed below the *base price equivalent* unless the resulting decrease in profits can be

recouped during periods of high volume through the establishment of prices correspondingly higher.
6. It must be recognized that capital normally enjoys a high rate of return in periods of high volume, and that higher prices at such times will intensify the attraction of competitive capital under speculative or ill-advised considerations.

PHASES OF THE PRICING PROBLEM

The method of analysis which has been outlined divides the pricing problem into the following parts:
1. Bearing upon the Matter of Policy:
   (a) The question of what has been described as the *economic return attainable,* representing the average annual rate of return which should be expected upon capital employed.
   (b) The question of capital requirement, which may be said to qualify the consideration of policy.
2. Bearing upon the Matter of Administrative Procedure:
   The question of the application of the *base price.* This may be said to afford the co-ordinating link between questions of policy and of administrative procedure.

A clear appreciation of the individual character and, at the same time, interdependence of these phases of the problem has important results. It facilitates two things:
1. Organized contact with conditions, and interpretation of them, leading to an intelligent enunciation of policy.
2. Effective exercise of authority, within appropriate bounds, on the part of executives engaged in the direct conduct of business.

The supply of capital, whether from retention of earnings or from sale of securities, is dependent upon the promise of a satisfactory rate of return, which in turn is determined by the profit margin in relationship to capital turnover. This relationship is symbolized by the *base price.* A deviation in prevailing price from the *base price equivalent* may afford a practical demonstration that a previously assumed *economic return attainable* is erroneous, and thus lead to a limitation upon the supply of capital for expansion. This method of price analysis, therefore, supplies the basis of a pricing policy which is the embodiment of a financial policy.

III—ILLUSTRATION OF METHOD OF ANALYSIS

Ordinarily prices cannot be fixed according to mathematical rule, or at figures calculated to yield a predetermined rate of return upon capital employed. Competitive conditions and other practical considerations are more apt to determine the prices which should be established, with the result that actual prices will rarely coincide exactly with the theoretical prices in accordance with an expressed pricing policy. This fact, however, does not mean that the expression of policy loses its significance; on the contrary, it makes clear the importance of interpreting the conditions which lead to apparent departure from the expressed policy, with a view to determining whether a modification of policy is required, or whether the conditions are of temporary import.

The availability of additional capital for expansion is dependent upon an expectation of the average rate of return obtainable. If actual conditions, as interpreted, demonstrate that a previously expected average rate of return upon capital employed in a given operation is no longer obtainable, the result may be a deliberate restriction upon further expansion, or even a curtailment of volume with release of capital for employment in more profitable channels. The analysis of price is just as important from the standpoint of indicating the rate of return obtainable upon capital employed as from the standpoint of determining the prices which should be established upon the product. The method of price analysis described in the preceding articles has the important attribute of segregating questions of policy from those of administration, and of facilitating the analysis and interpretation of price as bearing fundamentally upon matters of financial control.

The formulation of the pricing policy must be with regard to the particular circumstances pertaining to each individual business and to the industry of which it is a part, and generally is a matter of broad business judgment. When formulated it is expressed simply in the conception of what have been defined as *standard volume* and the *economic return attainable*. The question of the percentage of practical annual capacity which shall be set as *standard volume* must be dependent upon considerations such as the magnitude of annual sales volume fluctuations over a period of years commonly known as a business cycle, the extent of seasonal fluctuations in sales likely within years of large volume, the policy of the company with respect to seasonal accumulation of finished or semifinished product with a view of leveling the production curve, the necessity or desirability of maintaining excess plant capacity for emergency use, and kindred matters. The question of the *economic return attainable* is dependent upon many factors which come to a focus in the broad judgment of executives as to the highest rate of return which can be obtained on capital, consistent with a healthy growth of the business.

The application of the method of price analysis results in the determination of what has been defined as the *base price,* stated as a ratio or percentage of factory cost. The *base price* applied to the accounted factory cost of product determines what is known as the *base price equivalent,* which represents, theoretically, the price which should be established on the product to accord with the expressed policy. In the process of price fixing, this theoretical price should be set forth, and where the actual established price differs from the same there should be a clear understanding of the reasons leading to such deviation.

There is no hard and fast rule by which prices can be fixed, which would be uniformly applicable in a variety of cases. The *method of price analysis* outlined, however, is uniformly applicable, and may be illustrated by the following hypothetical figures. To simplify the matter, the statements are drawn up on the supposition that there is but one product of manufacture, and that its price is in exact agreement with the theoretical price.

For the purpose of illustration it will be supposed that the pricing policy is expressed by the following:

Standard Volume = 80 per cent of practical annual capacity.

Economic Return Attainable = 20 per cent on capital employed.

This is a complete expression of the policy, and simply means that, generally speaking, prices are to be established from time to time for the product which will yield an average annual rate of return, over a long period of time, of 20 per cent on capital employed in the business, provided the plants or factories operate at an average of 80 per cent of annual capacity.

Standard Volume Equivalent. In the application of the method of price analysis, *standard volume* must be reduced to its equivalent in physical volume, expressed either in units of product, tonnage, or value of plant output. With each increase of plant capacity there may be no change in *standard volume* as the expression of policy, but there will be a corresponding increase in the *standard volume equivalent* as representing physical volume. For the purposes of this illustration it will be supposed there is a plant of rated capacity and *standard volume equivalent* as in Table 6.

TABLE 6. PLANT CAPACITY AND STANDARD VOLUME EQUIVALENT

Daily Production Capacity	225 Units
Theoretical Annual Production Capacity (280 working days)	63,000 Units
Practical Annual Capacity (allowing for machine shut-downs, seasonal fluctuations in shipments, etc.)	50,000 Units
Standard Volume	80 Per cent
Standard Volume Equivalent	40,000 Units

Standard Factory Burden. It is assumed that Table 7 represents an analysis of manufacturing expense at various volumes.

The *standard volume equivalent* has been stated as 40,000 units. Manufacturing expense is absorbed in the factory cost of product on this basis at all volumes of production. Thus, if manufacturing expense is absorbed, as factory burden, on the basis of productive labor the standard burden rate will be 166-2/3 per cent, which will be applied at all times. Similarly the factory burden absorbed in the accounted cost will be $250 per unit regardless of what the volume of production might be at a given time. In this way there will be overabsorbed and unabsorbed burden, Table 8, at the various volumes.

TABLE 7. ANALYSIS OF MANUFACTURING EXPENSE AT VARIOUS VOLUMES

Item	Amount			
			(Standard Volume)	
Annual Rate of Production—Units	55,000	50,000	40,000	30,000
Productive Labor	$ 8,250,000	$ 7,500,000	$ 6,000,000	$4,500,000
Manufacturing Expenses:				
Fixed Expenses	2,000,000	2,000,000	2,000,000	2,000,000
Partially Controllable Expenses	9,325,000	8,750,000	7,600,000	6,450,000
Controllable Expenses	550,000	500,000	400,000	300,000
Total Manufacturing Expense	$11,875,000	$11,250,000	$10,000,000	$8,750,000
Ratio of Manufacturing Expense to Productive Labor	1.439	1.50	1.66⅔	1.944
Manufacturing Expense per Unit	$215.91	$225.00	$250.00	$291.67

The overabsorbed or unabsorbed burden is carried directly to the income account.

TABLE 8. OVERABSORBED AND UNABSORBED BURDEN AT THE VARIOUS VOLUMES

Item	Amount			
			(Standard Volume)	
Annual Rate of Production—Units	55,000	50,000	40,000	30,000
Burden, Per Unit, Absorbed in Accounted Cost	$250.00	$250.00	$250.00	$250.00
Total Burden Absorbed	13,750,000	12,500,000	10,000,000	7,500,000
Actual Burden	11,875,000	11,250,000	10,000,000	8,750,000
Overabsorbed Burden	$ 1,875,000	$ 1,250,000	. . . .	. . . .
Unabsorbed Burden	. . . .	. . . .	. . . .	$1,250,000

Factory Cost of Product. It is supposed that fluctuations of volume will not serve to alter the raw material cost and the productive labor cost per unit of product, and that accounted cost will be as in Table 9.

Standard Commercial Expense. It is customary to allow for commercial expense as a given percentage of annual sales. Table 10 represents an analysis of commercial expenses at various volumes.

TABLE 9. ACCOUNTED COST PER UNIT OF PRODUCT

Item	Factory Cost per Unit of Product
Raw Materials	$ 600
Productive Labor	150
Burden, at Standard Rate	250
Total Factory Cost, as Accounted	$1,000

Annual sales of 40,000 units representing standard volume, with commercial expenses at 7.0 per cent, it follows that this is the *standard allowance*. Actual commercial expenses are charged to operations.

TABLE 10. ANALYSIS OF COMMERCIAL EXPENSES AT VARIOUS VOLUMES

Item	Amount		(Standard Volume)	
Annual Sales, Units	55,000	50,000	40,000	30,000
Annual Sales, Value	$68,750,000	$62,500,000	$50,000,000	$37,500,000
Commercial Expenses:				
Fixed Expenses	$ 1,600,000	$ 1,600,000	$ 1,600,000	$ 1,600,000
Partially Controllable Expenses	$ 1,525,000	$ 1,450,000	$ 1,300,000	$ 1,150,000
Controllable Expenses	825,000	750,000	600,000	450,000
Total Commercial Expense	$ 3,950,000	$ 3,800,000	$ 3,500,000	$ 3,200,000
Per Cent of Annual Sales	5.75	6.08	7.0	8.53

Standard Fixed Investment Ratio. The standard fixed investment ratio is readily obtained, once standard volume and standard cost have been determined:

Investment in Plant, Equipment, and Real Estate $= \$15,000,000$
Standard Volume $=$ 40,000 units
Fixed Investment per unit of Product at Standard Volume $=$ \$375
Factory Cost of Product per unit $=$ \$1,000

Standard of Fixed Investment $= \dfrac{\$375}{\$1,000} =$ 0.375 of Annual Factory Cost

Working Capital Ratios. Other capital requirements are of variable character and will be in proportion to volume of business. Standards are established for these, Table 11, and are expressed as ratios to factory cost, or to sales, on an annual basis, according to whether the item is more directly related to costs or to sales value.

TABLE 11. STANDARDS EXPRESSED AS RATIOS TO FACTORY COST, OR TO SALES, ON AN ANNUAL BASIS

ITEM	STANDARDS	
	Ratio to Sales Annual Basis	Ratio to Factory Cost Annual Basis
Cash..	0.050	.....
Drafts and Accounts Receivable..................	0.100	.....
Raw Material and Work in Process...............	.....	0.16⅔
Finished Product...............................	.....	0.08⅓
Gross Working Capital......................	0.150	0.250

Base Price. The pricing policy having been expressed, and standards having been established for all expense and investment items, expressed as ratios to sales or to factory cost (depending upon the directness of the relationship), the *base price* can be readily determined. To arrive at the *base price* it is necessary only to apply the standard ratios and percentages referred to above, as illustrated in Table 12.

Base Price Equivalent and List Price. With the factory cost established as $1,000 per unit, the *base price equivalent* would be 125 per cent of $1,000 or $1,250, which figure represents the selling price *(net to company)* in conformity with the *base price*.

If the average discount to dealers is 20 per cent, the retail list price in conformity with the *base price* would be $\frac{\$1,250}{0.80}$ = $1,562.50.

The retail list price in conformity with *base price* may also be stated as $\frac{125 \text{ per cent}}{0.80}$, or 156.25 per cent, of factory cost (156.25 per cent of $1,000) or $1,562.50.

Non-Controllable Expenses at Different Volumes of Production. Since manufacturing expenses and commercial expenses do not increase or decrease in direct proportion to changes in volume of

TABLE 12. APPLICATION OF STANDARD RATIOS AND PERCENTAGES TO ARRIVE AT BASE PRICE

	STANDARDS		
ITEM	Ratio to Sales (Annual Basis)	Ratio to Factory Cost (Annual Basis)	Ratio to Sales[1] (Annual Basis)
1. Cash	0.050		0.050
2. Drafts and Accounts Receivable	0.100		0.100
3. Raw Material and Work in Process		0.16⅔	0.13⅓
4. Finished Product		0.08⅓	0.06⅔
5. Gross Working Capital	0.150	0.250	0.350
6. Fixed Investment		0.375	0.300
7. Total Investment	0.150	0.625	0.650
8. Standard Economic Return Attainable—20 Per Cent			
9. Final Net Profit (7 x 8)	0.030	0.125	0.130
10. Standard Commercial Expense—7 Per Cent	0.070		0.070
11. Gross Margin on Factory Cost	0.100 a	0.125 b	0.200

$$\text{Base Price, net to company} = \frac{(1+b)}{(1-a)} = \frac{1.+0.125}{1.-0.10} = \frac{1.125}{0.90} = 1.25 = \text{Ratio}$$
of base price (net to company) to factory cost

Therefore, Base Price = 125 per cent of factory cost.

---

[1] These ratios are easily arrived at after determining the *base price*, by carrying forward the ratios in column 1 without alteration, and the ratios in column 2 after dividing by the *base price*.

business, estimates of profits at varying volumes of business must take into account the degree of variability or controllability of these expenses, in order that the percentage of net profit to sales may be calculated. Similarly, that portion of the investment referred to as "Fixed Investment" (Real Estate, Plants, and Equipment, etc.) is constant regardless of the volume of business transacted, and influences the percentage earned on capital employed. Table 13 illustrates the non-controllability of manufacturing expenses and commercial expenses. Thus there is a uniform indication of a total amount of expense which is independent of volume of business ("non-controllable expense") in the amount of $7,300,000. The cost of doing business, per unit of product or as a percentage of sales, will vary as between different volumes by reason of this non-controllable expense. Sales at *standard volume* are $50,000,000, so that the indicated non-controllable expense is 14.6 per cent of sales at *standard volume*. Net profits at *standard*

TABLE 13. NON-CONTROLLABILITY OF MANUFACTURING EXPENSES AND COMMERCIAL EXPENSES

Item	Amount			
			(Standard Volume)	
Various Volumes of Business Under Observation, Units	55,000	50,000	40,000	30,000
Per cent of Standard Volume	137.5%	125%	100%	75%
Aggregate Mfg. Expense (Table 7)	$11,875,000	$11,250,000	$10,000,000	$ 8,750,000
Aggregate Commercial Expense (Table 10)	3,950,000	3,800,000	3,500,000	3,200,000
Aggregate Combined Expense	$15,825,000	$15,050,000	$13,500,000	$11,950,000
If the Expenses were Directly Proportionate to Volume, the Aggregate at the Indicated Volumes Would Be	18,562,500	16,875,000	13,500,000	10,125,000
The Difference Reflects the Non-controllable Character of the Expenses	$ 2,737,500	$ 1,825,000	....	$ 1,825,000
If This Difference be Divided by the Percentage Variance from Standard Volume, Which Is	37.5%	25%	....	25%
The Amount of Non-controllable Expense is Indicated as	$ 7,300,000	$ 7,300,000	....	7,300,000 $

volume are 13 per cent of net sales, so that the sales dollar at standard volume may be subdivided as in Table 14.

TABLE 14. SUBDIVISION OF THE SALES DOLLAR AT STANDARD VOLUME

Item	Per cent of Sales at Standard Volume
Non-controllable Expense, as Indicated Above	14.6
Net Profit, as Shown in Table 12	13.0
Combined Total	27.6
Variable Cost and Expense	72.4
Total Sales	100.00

At a given selling price the combined total of non-controllable expense and net profit will remain constant as a percentage of sales. With sales below *standard volume,* the percentage of non-controllable expense will be proportionately higher and the percentage of net profit correspondingly lower, and *vice versa* with sales above *standard volume*. For example:

With Sales at 137.5 per cent of Standard Volume,
Net Profit will equal 27.6 per cent $- \frac{14.6 \text{ per cent}}{1.375} = 16.98$ per cent of sales

With Sales at 125 per cent of Standard Volume,
Net Profit will equal 27.6 per cent $- \frac{14.6 \text{ per cent}}{1.25} = 15.92$ per cent of sales

With Sales at Standard Volume,
Net Profit will equal 27.6 per cent $- \frac{14.6 \text{ per cent}}{1.00} = 13.00$ per cent of sales

With Sales at 75 per cent of Standard Volume,
Net Profit will equal 27.6 per cent $- \frac{14.6 \text{ per cent}}{0.75} = 8.13$ per cent of sales

It will be noted that these profit percentages are in exact agreement with the figures shown in the summary tabulation, Table 15.

Return on Investment at Different Volumes. As the non-controllable expenses influence the profit margin, so the fixed portion of the investment influences the rate of return on capital. It is therefore not possible to compare directly the rate of return on capital actually realized or expected with the *economic return attainable*, since the latter represents an average rate of return to be realized over a period including both good and poor years, and is not the rate to be aimed at in a given year. In good years plants will operate at a rate in excess of *standard volume*, while in lean years they will operate at a lower rate. In years of high volume, the same *base price* will result in a rate of return on capital in excess of the *economic return attainable*, and in years of low volume in a rate of return smaller than the *economic return attainable*. Under the assumptions already employed, if operations were at the rate of 125 per cent of *standard volume*, the rate of return on capital at the *base price* would be 26.98 per cent, compared with 20 per cent at *standard volume*. On the other hand, if operations were curtailed to 75 per cent of *standard volume*, the rate of return would be only 10.84 per cent. It is essential, therefore, to be able to calculate readily the return on capital at different volumes of business at the *base price;* in other words, to determine what may be called the *standard return* at various volumes with which actual or expected return may be compared.

Summary Tabulation. Table 15 presents in summary form figures pertaining to profits, capital employed, and return on capital at the four different volumes of business previously considered.

STANDARDS SUBJECT TO EXAMINATION AND MODIFICATION

The standard ratios and percentages developed for price analysis should be compared currently with the actual ratios and percentages. Variations of actual figures from the standards are to be

TABLE 15. PROFITS, CAPITAL EMPLOYED, AND RETURN ON CAPITAL.
(At Four Different Volumes of Business)

Item	Amount				(Standard Volume)			
	55,000 $1,250	Ratio to Sales	50,000 $1,250	Ratio to Sales	40,000 $1,250	Ratio to Sales	30,000 $1,250	Ratio to Sales
Annual Sales, Units............	55,000	......	50,000	......	40,000	......	30,000	......
Net Selling Price Per Unit........	$1,250	......	$1,250	......	$1,250	......	$1,250	......
PROFIT AND LOSS STATEMENT:								
Annual Sales, Amount............	$68,750,000	1.000	$62,500,000	1.000	$50,000,000	1.000	$37,500,000	1.000
Factory Cost of Sales............	55,000,000	0.800	50,000,000	0.800	40,000,000	0.800	30,000,000	0.800
Gross Factory Profit.............	13,750,000	0.200	12,500,000	0.200	10,000,000	0.200	7,500,000	0.200
Commercial Expense.............	3,950,000	0.0575	3,800,000	0.0608	3,500,000	0.0700	3,200,000	0.0853
Net Profit Before Application of Overabsorbed or Unabsorbed Burden.......	9,800,000	0.1425	8,700,000	0.1392	6,500,000	0.1300	4,300,000	0.1147
Overabsorbed Burden............	1,875,000	0.0273	1,250,000	0.0200	......	......	......	......
Unabsorbed Burden.............	......	......	......	......	......	......	1,250,000	0.0200
Actual Net Profit................	$11,675,000	0.1698	$ 9,950,000	0.1592	$ 6,500,000	0.1300	$ 3,050,000	0.0813
CAPITAL EMPLOYED:		Ratio to Sales		Ratio to Sales		Ratio to Sales		Ratio to Sales
Cash..........................	$ 3,437,500	0.0500	$ 3,125,000	0.0500	$ 2,500,000	0.0500	$ 1,875,000	0.0500
Drafts and Accounts Receivable...	6,875,000	0.1000	6,250,000	0.1000	5,000,000	0.1000	3,750,000	0.1000
Raw Material and Work in Process..	9,167,000	0.1333	8,333,000	0.1333	6,167,000	0.1333	5,000,000	0.1333
Finished Product................	4,583,000	0.0667	4,167,000	0.0667	3,333,000	0.0667	2,500,000	0.0667
Gross Working Capital..........	$24,062,500	0.3500	$21,875,000	0.3500	$17,500,000	0.3500	$13,125,000	0.3500
Fixed Investment................	15,000,000	0.2182	15,000,000	0.2400	15,000,000	0.3000	15,000,000	0.4000
Total Investment............	$39,062,500	0.5682	$36,875,000	0.5900	$32,500,000	0.6500	$28,125,000	0.7500
RETURN ON CAPITAL EMPLOYED (annual rate), Per cent.	29.89		26.98		20.00		10.84	

expected, and may result from one or more of a variety of causes, as for example:

1. Normal seasonal accumulation of finished product carried in stock.

2. Temporary lack of balance in productive inventories due to transportation tie-ups, machine breakdowns, or other causes.
3. Unusually heavy commercial expenses due to intensive sales campaigns.

These would constitute temporary variances and would not necessitate a revision of standards. On the other hand, variances might exist by reason of changes of permanent character, such as the following:

1. Increased fixed investment ratio due to the construction of additional plant for the purpose of manufacturing parts previously purchased from outside sources of supply.
2. Increased inventory ratio due to a change in policy with regard to carrying finished product in inventory, or to permanent changes in transportation conditions, or in relations with suppliers.

Such changes would require a revision of the related standards and should be anticipated when possible.

Since *standard volume* and *economic return attainable* play so important a part in the analysis of price, a continuing observation of all conditions involved in their determination is essential.

Price in Relation to Financial Control

While competitive conditions and other practical considerations ordinarily are the chief determinants of the price which shall be charged for a product, nevertheless comprehensive financial policies are necessary in business organizations which employ large amounts of capital. The pronouncement of a basic pricing policy, in terms of the *economic return* attainable, should be understandable *as a policy*, and should not be misapplied as a dictation of specific price. In other words, the impracticability of frequent adjustment of prices must be recognized, necessitating the maintenance of prices which at times may be above, and at other times below the *base price equivalent*. With due allowance for deviations of this nature, the method of price analysis affords a means not only of interpreting actual or proposed prices in relation to the established policy, but at the same time affords a practical demonstration as to whether the policy itself is sound. If the prevailing price of product is found to be at variance with the *base price equivalent*, other than to the the extent due to temporary causes, it must follow that prices should be adjusted; or else, in the event of conditions being such that prices cannot be brought into line with the *base price equivalent*, the conclusion is necessarily drawn that the terms of the expressed policy must be modified.

It becomes apparent, therefore, that the analysis of price in accordance with the method outlined is closely interwoven with the matter of financial control, since the expression of price policy, in terms of rate of return attainable on capital employed, is the most significant factor bearing upon the question of availability of capital for purposes of operation.

A STATEMENT OF GENERAL MOTORS CORPORATION'S BASIC POLICIES GOVERNING ITS RELATIONS WITH FACTORY EMPLOYES

FOREWORD

Uniform policies governing General Motors industrial relations are essential to the success of the Corporation and are consistent with its policy of decentralized operation.

The Divisional Managers are charged with the responsibility for maintaining satisfactory employe relations, and the enunciation of the Corporation's basic policies is intended as an aid in fulfilling this responsibility.

The basic principles and policies herein set forth are to govern relations with factory employes throughout the various Divisions of the General Motors Corporation. All explicit instructions or conditions herein set forth must be observed and special care must be exercised that there be no violation with respect to those conditions whose observance is specifically required under the law or the accepted interpretations thereof.

Although the policies and principles enunciated herein are directed toward the governing of relations with factory employes, nevertheless there is a great deal of the philosophy underlying these policies and principles which should be equally applicable to employes outside of that category.

I

INTRODUCTION

The Management of General Motors holds that there is no real conflict of interests between employers and employes. Such apparent conflicts as arise may usually, if not indeed always, be traceable to a lack of mutual understanding or to a shortsighted viewpoint on the one side or the other. Enlightened employers and enlightened employes realize that they have a mutuality of interests such as to dictate the wisdom of maintaining the highest degree of co-operation and harmonious relations.

General Motors is a part of an industry where there has long been a natural regard for, and understanding of, the benefits which flow from a high general standard of living—that is, from widely diffused high real wages and real incomes. All industry is ultimately, and the automobile industry is directly, dependent upon the ability as well as the desire of consumers to buy. Wage and salary employes represent a great mass of consumers, whose buying power rests upon the wages and salaries they derive from industry and trade. This is a relationship between business in general and workers in general as consumers of industry's products.

There is another relationship, however, between the management of any particular business and its employes, which is a more direct and intimate one. This relationship requires a harmonious working together to the end that the quality and cost of the product may be such that the business will prove continuingly successful and will survive.

The management of General Motors is conscious of the fact that it cannot get along without labor any more than labor can get along without management. Both are in the same business and the success of that business is vital to all concerned. At times the employes and the management may have different ideas as to various matters affecting their relationship. This divergence of ideas may result from lack of understanding and in such instances may be cleared up through some process which brings about a mutual comprehension of each other's problems.

Employer-employe relations are human relations and they cannot be perfected without common understanding. On the side of management there might be the failure to take advantage of the mutual supervisory contacts in conveying to employes an understanding of management's aims and purposes. Likewise there might be a lack of understanding by management of the employes' viewpoints. On the employes' side it may be that recognized representatives of the employes fail to have, or to convey to the management, complete understanding of the employes' viewpoint, or fail to transmit to the body of employes an understanding of the management's viewpoint. Under such conditions there are weaknesses which interfere with the accurate intercommunication of ideas and viewpoints required to achieve the mutual understanding essential to continuing harmonious relations.

The philosophy and policies of General Motors are such that it should be possible to achieve this harmonious relationship. It is the duty of every element of the management to accept the philosophy and principles enunciated in this statement of policy and to be guided thereby in all dealings with employes. The management is convinced that, given sincere and patient effort on both sides, there is no reason why problems arising out of relationships with employes cannot be satisfactorily adjusted within the organization.

In the establishment and maintenance of an effective working relationship between management and employes under which the rights and interests of each may be mutually understood and kept in equitable adjustment, employe representation for purposes of collective bargaining may have an important place, although this of itself will not necessarily insure the mutual understanding and co-operative attitude essential to maintaining the most satisfactory relations. The objective can be fully served only by having that sympathetic intercommunication already referred to, where there is understanding by the management of the employes' point of view as developed from intelligent thought on the latter's part, and understanding by the employes as a whole of the aims and purposes of the management. If a system of employe representation can be devised to serve these purposes, it will prove highly beneficial to all.

II

SCOPE OF COLLECTIVE BARGAINING AS APPLYING IN GENERAL MOTORS

Collective bargaining is to be understood as a method of intercommunication and negotiation between employes and management whose objective is the maintenance of harmonious and cooperative relations through mutual understanding and agreement with respect to terms and conditions of employment. It may be practiced informally as well as formally. But when there are specific and generally understood provisions for the handling of all matters coming within its scope, and when there is a clearly defined management policy with respect to relations with employes, the groundwork will have been established for fostering mutual understanding and co-operation.

It is important in the beginning to define as exactly as possible the limits within which management can agree to compose differences with employes, and beyond which it cannot go without surrendering its responsibility.

Management should recognize the importance of social considerations as influencing broad policies governing industrial relations. For example, if medical research discovers that certain conditions of employment are inimical to the health of the employes, management should take such action as is practicable to remedy the harmful conditions.

On the other hand, management has certain inherent responsibilities and duties which must also be recognized.

The fact that management subscribes to the principles of collective bargaining in no way absolves management of such inherent duties, nor has management the right to relinquish such responsibilities. It must be made clear that collective bargaining does not imply the assumption by the employe of a voice in those affairs of management which management, by its very nature, must ultimately decide upon its own responsibility. It does not mean collective employer-employe management and must be limited to employer-employe relationships.

Management is charged with the responsibility for promoting and maintaining the best long-term interests of the business as a continuing institution. Therefore, while management should exhaust every means in endeavoring to settle all problems of employer-employe relations which may arise, it cannot agree to submit to arbitration (which is a surrender by both sides to the authority of an outside agency) any point at issue where compromise might injure the long-term interests of the business and therefore, in turn, damage the mass of employes themselves.

This does not in any way mean that impartial or judicial agencies have no place in collective bargaining. On the contrary, controversial questions of *fact*, such as discrimination cases and questions of lay-off, may frequently be more amicably and speedily settled through an impartial, competent, fact-finding agency having the confidence of both sides.

It is important to insure compliance with the Corporation's policy governing those questions which, when necessary, may be submitted to outside arbitration or mediation, as distinguished from those questions resting essentially upon managerial responsibility. Therefore, instructions are hereby laid down that no case is to be submitted to the determination of any outside agency without the specific authorization of the Executive Committee.

Finally, collective bargaining, by its very nature, implies an effort to reach a satisfactory agreement and is not fulfilled when the management merely listens to the proposals of employes or their representatives and rejects them. The responsibility rests on *both* sides to make every reasonable effort to compose any difference of opinion.

III

COLLECTIVE BARGAINING PROCEDURE

Membership in a labor union or other type of labor or employe organization does not in itself establish the right of any such union or other organization to represent employes in collective bargaining negotiations. Representatives for such purpose must have been specifically chosen by the employes they are to represent and the fact of such choice must be established.

While there is the technical requirement that in collective bargaining negotiations the right to represent employes must be duly established, nevertheless the management should be reasonable in its willingness to listen to anyone desiring to discuss matters purporting to affect General Motors employes.

A. UNDERSTANDINGS RESULTING FROM NEGOTIATIONS

In the event that an issue is raised by a particular group or their duly accredited representatives, the settlement of which involves the interests of non-represented groups, the management should satisfy itself that any decision arrived at provides fair treatment with respect to such non-represented groups.

B. PROCEDURE WITH BARGAINING GROUPS

   1. *Questions Not Requiring Formal Conference*

      The procedure outlined in this sub-section does not contemplate formal conferences between management and employes or their representatives, but rather the ordinary managerial consideration and attention to views and contentions indicated in behalf of employes. Questions raised be employes, or by accredited representatives, should be dealt with as expeditiously as practicable at all times.

      Experience indicates that many questions and problems brought up for consideration by employes or their representatives can be settled to advantage by the foreman. The foreman, by the very nature of his position is the representative of men to management, as well as of management to men. He is in a position of authority to take action on matters brought to his attention and to refer matters outside his authority to his superiors. Moreover, the solution of questions and problems within the line organization generally brings the most satisfactory long-term results to both employes and to management. Routine matters falling within the scope of authority of the foreman or the supervisory executive in immediate contact, should be settled on the spot whenever it is possible to arrive at a satisfactory understanding. When the matter is outside of the scope of the authority of the foreman or the supervisory executive in immediate contact, or if a satisfactory settlement cannot be made by him, the foreman or the executive should in all cases submit the matter to his superior. Similarly, if the matter is outside of the scope of authority of the executive to whom it has been submitted, or if he cannot settle it satisfactorily, he, in turn, should submit it to his superior and successively the matter should be referred up through the organization until it reaches the executive whose scope of authority enables him to make final decision. Every effort should be made to effect an amicable settlement, even if this necessitates referring the matter all the way up to the General Manager of the Division. When a matter has been decided, not only the exact nature of the decision, but also the management's viewpoint thereon, should be made clear to those down the line to the point of initial contact with the matter.

   2. *Questions Requiring Formal Conference*

      In all matters which cannot be settled informally and with mutual understanding, and which justify conference to reconcile opposing viewpoints, it is necessary to give practical consideration to the requirements of the case. With the general duties and responsibilities resting upon the supervisory executives, it is impracticable for them to hold themselves in readiness for conference with employes or their representatives at any time the occasion might present itself. Each Division should establish a definite plan providing that a conference will be held within five days from the receipt of written notice setting forth the purpose for which conference is desired.

The principal resident executive should, if possible, participate in these conferences.

3. *Records of Meetings for Purposes of Collective Bargaining*

Each Division shall keep an adequate record of all meetings with properly accredited representatives of its employes, including the terms of understanding entered into by the management, so as to minimize any conflict of interpretations.

In order that the Corporation may be fully informed with respect to the manner in which the collective bargaining efforts of each Division are proceeding, EACH DIVISION SHALL REPORT THROUGH ITS GROUP EXECUTIVE TO THE EXECUTIVE VICE-PRESIDENT ALL CASES WHICH HAVE BEEN RAISED AND AS TO WHICH THE DIVISION MANAGEMENT HAS BEEN UNABLE TO REACH A SATISFACTORY SETTLEMENT WITH EMPLOYES OR THEIR REPRESENTATIVES WITHIN TWO WEEKS FROM DATE OF INCEPTION. In submitting such reports, the Division should include complete details of the cases involved.

4. *Appeal Procedure for Employes or Employe Representatives*

In any case where it has not been possible to arrive at an amicable understanding through conference and discussion—even after the case has been referred to the General Manager of the Division—employes or their representatives may refer the case to the Department of Industrial Relations in Detroit. In such cases a complete statement of the facts, together with supporting evidence, should be submitted by both sides to the controversy.

The Department of Industrial Relations will review the material submitted and make such independent investigations as may be necessary to determine if there has been either a violation of company policies or if the case involves matter beyond the scope of divisional authority.

If it is found that the case falls within either of the above two categories, the complete facts will be referred to the Executive Vice-President through the group executive for such action as may be required.

The Executive Vice-President will, for the information of the Executive Committee, make a report to it on all such appeal cases referred to him.

5. *Subjects for Discussion*

Under the conditions outlined herein, the management of each Division will provide means whereby any question subject to collective bargaining raised by employes may be discussed and endeavor made to reach a satisfactory settlement thereof.

It must be distinctly understood that it is contrary to the letter and the spirit of collective bargaining for the management to attempt by any means to prevent questions as regards same from being raised by the employes and fully discussed with them or their representatives.

C. RELATIONS WITH EMPLOYE COLLECTIVE BARGAINING ORGANIZATIONS

Employes must be given entire freedom with respect to the selection and form and rules of their organization and their selection of representatives.

This principle does not preclude the management from assisting or advising any employe organization in the development or carrying out of plans for the employes' mutual benefit, provided that in the determination of the right of employes to participate in any benefits resulting from such activities there be no discrimination by management on the ground of affiliation or non-affiliation with any employe or labor organization.

D. SOLICITATION ON COMPANY PREMISES

The President's Automobile Settlement states:

"The Government makes it clear that it favors no particular union or particular form of employe organization or representation. The Government's only duty is to secure absolute and uninfluenced freedom of choice without coercion, restraint, or intimidation from any source."

Since this provision bans coercion by unions as well as employers, all cases of attempted coercion to force employes to join labor organizations should be thoroughly investigated and if they can be substantiated, referred through the lines of organization to the Industrial Relations Department in Detroit for their records and such use as may be found desirable.

No solicitation of membership in any employe or labor organization, or any other kind of organization, is to be permitted on Company premises. This rule must be impartially enforced without discrimination.

IV
INCREASING AND REDUCING LABOR FORCES

The law is explicit in its provision that no one seeking employment shall be required as a condition of employment to join any employes' association or to refrain from joining, organizing or assisting a labor organization of his own choosing.

It is important that all Employment Departments make every effort to hire local employes. Only after all satisfactory available local applicants have been hired should employment be given applicants from other communities. When the addition of employes for limited periods of seasonal or other peak employment could be avoided, if the existing labor force were permitted to work more than the normal schedule of hours, it should be done so as to avoid the economic and social consequences which result from the addition of temporary employes for brief periods of employment.

In the lay-off and rehiring of employes, divisional management will be governed by the rules in effect as of May 25, 1935, which give due weight to marital status, dependents, length of service, skill and efficiency, and such interpretations of these rules as have been or may be hereafter approved by the Executive Vice-President.

V
DISCHARGE OF EMPLOYES

The management has the full right to discharge an employe for cause, such as, for example, insubordination, inefficiency, or infraction of shop rules. The decision to discharge an employe, however, must rest upon clear grounds and must be reasonable. Furthermore, the full reasons for discharge should be recorded and should be stated explicitly to the employe.

The law is explicit in its prohibition of discharging employes for affiliation or non-affiliation with any labor or employe organization or for joining, organizing, or assisting a labor organization of their own choosing.

The prohibition against discrimination places an additional responsibility upon the management to furnish clear evidence of the justification of the discharge of any employe in the event that discrimination is alleged.

Although no employe is to be discharged because of membership in a labor union or other organization, this does not mean that such membership confers any immunity from discharge for justifiable cause or in particular prevents the discharge of any employes who are trouble makers, as, for example, those who seek by violence, threats, sabotage, or obstructive acts, to coerce, intimidate, or interfere with fellow employes or the management. It must be clearly understood, however, that the charge of "trouble making" is not to be used as a subterfuge for discharging union members merely because they are union members.

It is one of the most immediate and vital responsibilities of the management of each Division to make these points clear to everyone in its supervisory organization, and the management must be held accountable in any case where discrimination is clearly apparent.

VI

INFORMING SEPARATED EMPLOYES OF THEIR STATUS

When a man is separated from any Division he should be given a release slip, clearly indicating the reasons. If he is discharged, he should know why; if laid off on account of reduction in force, it must be understood he is eligible for reemployment. When a man quits, his release slip should indicate this. The slip and the employment record should give the employe's status in plain English, not in code.

The foreman should be thoroughly familiar with all the facts.

ALFRED P. SLOAN, JR.
President
GENERAL MOTORS CORPORATION

Approved by

The Executive Committee
General Motors Corporation

July 26, 1934

Revised July 2, 1935

DECENTRALIZED OPERATIONS AND RESPONSIBILITIES WITH COORDINATED CONTROL

A typescript of a paper read before the Winter Convention of the American Management Association in the City of New York, February, 1927 by Donaldson Brown, Vice-president, General Motors Corporation

Reprinted by Permission of the Publisher. From the AMA Annual Convention Series, No. 57, © 1927 by American Management Association, Inc.

DECENTRALIZED OPERATIONS AND RESPONSIBILITIES
WITH COORDINATED CONTROL

A paper read before the Winter Convention
of the American Management Association in
the City of New York, February, 1927
By Donaldson Brown, Vice-President
General Motors Corporation

There is probably no subject relating to industrial management more important than this. Yet, I am told, very little has been written which deals with it in a comprehensive way. There is good reason for a hesitancy to lay down general rules. The problem involves theories of psychology on which there is no lack of authoritative references, but a practical application of such theories is circumscribed by the personal equation and peculiar circumstances in individual cases.

The invitation to present the paper comes to me, of course, because of my association with General Motors, a corporation employing approximately nine hundred million dollars of gross assets, something like 160,000 employes, and comprising a large number of separate and distinct operating divisions.

Among these separate divisions are the car divisions, owned directly and embracing Buick, Cadillac, Chevrolet, Oakland and Pontiac, and Oldsmobile, which are recognized as leaders or else among the largest automobile producers in their respective price fields. The Fisher Body group supplying automobile bodies to the car divisions, is now owned and operated as a division of General Motors and, in itself, is one of the largest businesses in the United States. Also there are numerous divisions manufacturing parts and accessories for automobiles, each one a highly specialized business and, in most cases, selling products in competitive markets as well as to our own car divisions.

Obviously, such a condition renders it impossible for General Motors to have a centralized organization in the sense of functional responsibilities. Each one of its divisions, from the standpoint of administrative management, has a fully self-contained organization, with a general manager responsible over all of the usual functional activities, such as engineering, purchasing production and sales; and including financial control. Yet, as an institution, having to account to its stockholders for constructive progress, General Motors must justify its corporate existence. There must be a sound measure of centralized control so as to assure the proper coordination of its various activities and the ability to capitalize, to the maximum degree, the great advantages derived from its combined size and importance in the industrial world.

1. Fundamental Principles of Management

It goes without saying that the experience of General Motors has only a limited application to most other businesses. Obviously, its problems differ materially from those of a less diversified business whose directing management is in immediate contact with all operations. There is a similarity of fundamental principles, however, and I shall be glad if a brief outline of our own experience may prove of use as introductory to further study.

I am going to take the liberty of first touching upon fundamental principles of management which are applicable to any industrial business today, in order to illustrate the adaptation of those principles in our particular circumstances.

All of us have a full appreciation of the importance of promoting initiative and enthusiastic effort down the line of organization by the delegation of authority and placement of responsibility. The difficulty in executive management is not in recognizing the advantages of placing responsibilities, but rather in distinguishing where limitations should be placed in order to gain necessary coordination.

By responsibility we mean the exercise of prerogatives, either implied or specifically assigned, the jurisdiction of an individual. Accountability would be a better word, for the individual who delegates authority does not divest himself of responsibility. The clerk has responsibilities which are assigned to him; the shop foreman has responsibilities under the jurisdiction and guidance of the shop superintendent; the general sales manager's responsible for sales, but he is expected to delegate authority to those under him and to hold each responsible in the performance of his assigned duties. Each department is responsible for the work in which it is engaged, and the exercise of this responsibility is served best by the assignment of authority and jurisdiction down the line as far as the capacity of the personnel will permit. Yet, there is the full responsibility upon the department head, and in turn the general manager, while the president is responsible over the whole. In the sense that each individual is responsible to someone superior, culminating through a series of lines of jurisdiction in the responsibility of the president himself, central control is absolutely essential as governing every activity in business management. This kind of control might be an ideal administrative control; and the proper assignment of duties and responsibilities down the line of organizational administrative management.

Men are jealous of their prerogatives. In fact, business management today has no high position for the man who lacks the courage of his convictions and who brooks interference with the duties and responsibilities which he knows to be within his rights. Promotion goes to the man who shows ability to assume responsibilities a little beyond the defined duties of his position, and the development of personnel and esprit de corps results from the delegation of authority and responsibility. But every man charged with responsibilities and vested with authority must be brought to realize that his function is tributary to the accomplishment of a central motive. To whatever degree this spirit can be engendered throughout the organization, to that degree the central motive itself becomes the controlling power. There is no occasion for resentment where the functional activities of an individual are guided in the direction of an ultimate purpose, the existence of which is made known and in the conception of which the responsibility is recognized as resting elsewhere.

Since business owes its existence to its owners, it is expected to operate for their benefit. This is not inconsistent with the broader ideas of service to the public, because it is only through service to the public that profits to the owners may be assured permanently. Thus there is just one central motive in industrial management, i.e., the permanent welfare of the owners of the business. This central motive or ultimate purpose is learned through the determination of what are known as policies. Such policies as it is possible to establish in clear cut terms must be laid down for the guidance of the administrative management. Unfortunately, it is impossible to pinpoint the character of all the varied problems that present themselves in management and to embrace them by a definite expression of policy the administrative management is none the less subservient to the policy viewpoint. Where doubt exists, those responsible for policies must be consulted and decisions of policy laid down.

In the true sense "centralized control" refers to the central motive of management. It requires that the activity of all departments be controlled so that they coordinate with the needs of the business, and with the requirements of policy. One-man control applied in the sense that one man dictates as to details of management is destructive to ultimate progress. But one-man control is essential as applied in the sense that he has a full appreciation of policy and a comprehensive knowledge of what is going on, to the end purpose.

If there is a complete coordination, with full regard to the permanent welfare of the owners of the business, then it follows that centralized control exists.

Most large businesses today are in the hands of corporations owned by scattered stockholders. The corporation has a board of directors. The directors, individually and collectively, have the responsibility to represent the interests of all the stockholders; in other words, to see that centralized control exists. Usually the board is comprised partially of men actively engaged in other directions, who cannot be in sufficiently close touch to exercise direct action in the determination of policies. This brings about the designation of a sub-committee, usually called the executive committee, comprised of board members more closely identified with the business, to whom broad authority is often delegated by the board.

But the board of directors has, and cannot evade, the sole duty of representing the stockholders. To the extent that discretionary power is left in the hands of an executive committee, it requires confidence and faith in the breadth of view and ability of that sub-group to exercise the prime function. There can be no shifting of the ultimate responsibility.

Just as in the case of the board of directors, where it is proper that broad authority be delegated to a sub-committee, so it is proper and advantageous to the stockholders that authority be conferred upon the administrative management as far as it is possible, so long as there is assurance of a proper degree of coordination, and compliance with what may be required from the standpoint of policy.

The fact that the board of directors, or we will say the executive committee acting for it, has the unescapable responsibility of centralized control does not mean that there should be committee management. If the executive committee be composed of department heads, or men actively engaged in the administrative management, it is usually advantageous because of their intimate knowledge of the problems of the business. On the other hand, this circumstance makes it difficult at times to distinguish between those questions requiring executive committee action and those questions which, in the interest of individual initiative, had better be left to administrative control. It should be recognized that the function of any individual as a member of the executive committee is quite different from his function as an executive officer. Committee action is by majority vote; executive action is by individual choice. The executive may seek the counsel and advice of any number of men on a given problem, but the decision is his. It matters not the extent to which he accepts the judgement of others, the action is his own individual responsibility. There is much truth in the saying that "what is everybody's business is nobody's business," and there can be no doubt that where committee action is applied to problems of purely administrative management it is almost always bad.

Having noted the necessity of centralized control and the responsibility of the executive committee in this regard, it is well to consider how its function can be exercised with no unwholesome effect upon the other phases of the management problem. The following may be laid down as the basis upon which the duties and responsibilities of the Executive Committee may be defined:

(1st) There must be a knowledge of the characteristics of the business and an understanding of the degree to which coordination exists or may be made to prevail through the cooperative activity of departments, operating under individual responsibilities and distinct lines of authority. Knowledge of the business and the use of statistical analyses suitably designed are essential to serve this first requisite.

(2nd) Wherever practicable, it is desirable to lay down a concrete policy as establishing the fundamental basis upon which the activity of any or all departments shall be predicated. This can be done only where it is possible to express a point of policy in clear terms capable of interpretation and proper application in the varied conditions that occur and with which the administrative management must contend.

(3rd) In the many cases where it is impossible to lay down any general rules and yet where the question of policy is no less involved, it becomes necessary to deal with problems as they arise. In this there is always the danger of encroaching upon the sphere of administrative management, and it is of great importance to analyze the characteristics of the problem so that it can be dealt with from the policy standpoint.

(4th) The President is the chief administrative officer and the connecting link between policy and administrative control. It has been stated that so long as complete coordination exists there is no need for the imposition of any central authority. The president must distinguish clearly between questions of policy and questions of administrative control applying to problems as they arise, and one of the most important functions of his position is to see that there is no undue interference with the prerogatives of individuals in the organization. Where there is any room for doubt as to what may be best for the welfare of the stockholders, he must secure from the executive committee an expression of policy. In all respects, it is the president's duty to see that coordination exists just as far as it is possible, and at the same time that those down the line have all the latitude and authority that is warranted, with a full sense of responsibility, so that there will be the greatest possible enthusiasm and exercise of initiative throughout the organization.

(5th)   In rare cases and under unusual circumstances, where it is impossible to draw the necessary distinction as to the line of policy, it may be justifiable for the executive committee to assume the responsibility of direct action in respect to matters of administrative character. This should be avoided, if possible, and always where such a course is necessary care should be taken to point out that the question of policy is involved and that it is impossible to secure a distinct separation of policy from questions of administrative responsibility admittedly included.

II   General Motors Type of Organization

In the case of the General Motors, the Board of Directors has two sub-committees; a Finance Committee responsible for general financial policies, and an Executive Committee responsible for operating policies.

The Finance Committee includes men of large affairs identified with banking and with big business, apart from General Motors, while the Executive Committee is composed of men giving all of their time to the affairs of General Motors. In a limited sense the Executive Committee is subject to the Finance Committee in that operations are dependent upon financial policies. At the same time, financial policies must be maintained so that operations will not be deprived of any legitimate development. Cooperation, as between these two committees, is furthered by the fact of common membership on the part of several individuals.

Obviously, it is humanly and physically impossible for the Executive Committee of General Motors to maintain the same kind of intimate contact with the details of its business as would be practicable in the case of a very much less diversified business. Still the responsibility to stockholders is exactly the same and the proper organization of control has been forced by absolute necessity. Otherwise, the business were better split up into various units with separate ownership, even at the sacrifice of the great advantages of the existing combination, so that the stockholders of each unit respectively could elect a board of directors capable of assuming the usual responsibilities. Let us examine, first, the general way in which the separate units of the Corporation are constituted.

Each one of these operating units, known as divisions, is entirely self-contained, with a general manager and complete jurisdiction and responsibility established.

There is never any conflict of jurisdiction, with respect to capital invested. Where any given plant produces a component entering into the finished product of just one of our divisions, it is deemed proper, unless the manufacture is of a highly specialized character, that the investment in that plant and its operation be placed under the jurisdiction of the consuming division. Generally speaking, where the product of a given plant enters into the product of two or more of our divisions, it is deemed desirable to place the investment in such plant and the full responsibility for its operation under the jurisdiction of a separately organized division. It is thus that our numerous parts and accessory divisions derive their separate entity.

Apart from certain distinct units embraced in the Fisher Body operations, we have fifteen divisions manufacturing components and accessories, such as ignition systems, bearings, gears, etc. These divisions are grouped together under the general guidance of a vice-president who is a member of the Executive Committee of General Motors.

All of these divisions are selling product to our car divisions, with the exception of one that is embraced in the group, which manufactures Frigidaires and farm lighting units. Also these divisions almost without exception sell product outside.

The question of pricing product from one division to another is of great importance. Unless a true competitive situation is preserved, as to prices, there is no basis upon which the performance of the divisions can be measured. No division is required absolutely to purchase product from another division. In their interrelation they are encouraged to deal just as they would with outsiders. The independent purchaser that is buying product from any of our divisions is assured that prices to it are exactly in line with prices charged our own car divisions. Where there are no substantial sales outside, such as would establish a competitive basis, the buying division determines the competitive picture- at times partial requirements are actually purchased from outside sources so as to perfect the competitive situation.

In the Fisher Body group are included separate and distinct units supplying materials such as lumber, glass, hardware, etc., for body construction. The interrelation of these units with the final body manufacture is exactly the same as that between the other divisions which I have described.

There are five automobile divisions in General Motors operating in the United States, each occupying a position in a distinct price class in the industry. There is charged to each the total investment in plants and other assets over which it has complete jurisdiction.

In addition there is a separate division handling the assembly and sale of all cars in Canada and an export group handling the sale of all cars in other foreign countries. This latter group has charge of assembly, as well, where cars are assembled abroad.

The general test of efficiency of management of any business is the rate of return on capital employed. Capital in industry is entitled to a varying rate of return largely dependent upon competitive conditions in the broad sense and the hazard that is involved. Needless to say good-will, that intangible and illusive, but none the less valuable, asset which every business seeks to enjoy is of great importance. Apart from this, however, profit from industry is dependent upon the character of product supplies and the degree of protection afforded by patents of specialized knowledge and skill in processes and methods of manufacture and distribution. At the same time the rate of return on capital is affected directly by the control of investment in working capital items and fixed assets in relation to the volume of business. Capital employed in the production and sale of a product that is bought on the basis of exact specifications, in the manufacture and distribution of which no highly specialized knowledge is required, contents itself with a relatively low rate of return. The production of an article that is exclusive in design, possessing superior engineering qualities and carrying with it a peculiar appeal to fashion or the taste of the public affords to capital the opportunity of enjoying a high rate of return. The hazard which always accompanies such a condition is minimized by the exercise of skill in progressive engineering improvements, and ingenuity in anticipating the changing tastes of the buying public. In gauging the effectiveness of management the first approach always is to examine the over-all result-the rate of return enjoyed on capital employed. If this be subnormal, having due regard to the character of business and the competitive situation, it is self-evident that something is wrong. The second step is to identify the cause.

With the segregation of General Motors into separate businesses of distinct classification we are in position to compare the performance of various divisions respectively with competition in the same line. Thus we can gauge the overall effectiveness of management in each case. By the use of suitable statistics and contact with the management of the various divisions, the president of the corporation and central group executives are able to detect instances of faulty control and to bring about the correction of a recognized condition by way of intelligent suggestion. The executive committee is able to deal with operating policies in respect to any division with an understanding of the characteristics of the particular business and the position of the division in its field of competition. This type of organization as applied to big business lends assistance to a high degree of centralized control, while at the same time it affords an opportunity of fixing responsibilities upon the administrative management on a clear-cut basis upon which they can be held accountable for results.

As a general proposition, I should say that in any business of considerable size and diversification, capable of being subdivided into units having the characteristics which I have described as pertaining to General Motors' divisions, such segregation is deserving of the most serious consideration. If the advantages of such a type of organization are to be enjoyed fully, it is absolutely essential that each unit be constituted so that it represents a self-contained business enterprise. The capital placed under its jurisdiction must be identified definitely with its own business and no other; and prices at which its products are sold must be based upon actual competitive values. Otherwise there is no tangible basis upon which the general effectiveness of the direct management can be gauged reliably.

This scheme of organization is usually referred to as the decentralized type. Opposed to this is the centralized type of organization, made up of functional departments; with an executive in charge of all manufacturing operations, another in charge of all sales, and with central purchasing and engineering departments. As to any of these functional activities it is difficult for anyone not in constant contact to judge the efficiency of performance even though he might have a specialized knowledge of the particular type of activity. With accurate accounting practices and painstaking analyses the manufacturing cost of a given component, or the complete product of manufacture, at times may be compared with the price at which a similar thing can be purchased elsewhere. However, it is very rare that a comparison can be had with the cost of manufacture elsewhere. Also it is impossible to arrive at a conclusive comparision of sales effectiveness and efficiency. Unrecognized inefficiency in manufacture may throw an impossible task upon a very efficient sales department. On the other hand an inefficient sales department may make it impossible to capitalize a highly economical manufactured product. In any event general managership is needed. This is essential, not only to gain proper coordination of functional activities, but from the standpoint of having some one in sufficiently close touch with details as to be competent to size up the effectiveness and efficiency of departmental management.

In the days of small business, corporations or privately owned businesses were managed by men who had a detailed knowledge of all the functional phases of the business. Department heads, and even those below had intimate contact with the general problems of the business, and gained knowledge in the essentials of general managership. The heads of many large corporations today had their early training in the atmosphere of the small business, and know from experience the character of problems which present themselves down the line and recognize the need and method of coordinating the various activities. In the sense in which I am using the phrase, there are still many small businesses. But a large share of the country's manufacturing business today is conducted by huge corporations, brought into being by force of economic developments and the opportunity of capitalizing the enormous advantages of large-scale operation. As applied to these there is a comparatively new problem of organization. That problem is to combine the economical advantages of modern business, with as little sacrifice as possible of that intimate control and development of managerial ability that is characteristic of the well managed small business.

Most of the divisions of General Motors are enormous in themselves, but separately they do not have the complication of products of highly diversified character or type. Operating as separate self-contained businesses, the divisions afford the advantages of concentrated management inherent in the small business. It has been pointed out that apart from these advantages, this scheme of organization facilitates the exercise of centralized control from the policy standpoint in the case of a corporation constituted as General Motors is.

Apart from the coordination of activities within each operating division, there are questions of corporation policy having to do with inter-divisional relations. There must be no undue conflict, competively, between the product of one division and that of another. There are certain general policies which, if good for one division, are good for all divisions. There are other questions of policy which must be determined from the standpoint of the corporation as a whole, rather than from the standpoint of any single division.

Purchases of materials must be conducted in a way so that the full advantages may be enjoyed from the combined requirements of all divisions. Engineering developments of fundamental character must be brought to light and the adaptability determined. Manufacturing methods and policies demonstrated to be advantageous in one place must be considered for adaptation under like conditions elsewhere. Similarly as to sales methods and policies. All products sold are advertised directly by the divisions respectively. However, General Motors advertises as an institution. The institutional advertising must be coordinated with the direct product advertising; and the integrity of the corporation's position must be preserved by making sure that the advertising is according to the facts, and in line with the policies of the corporation.

Serving in the direction of crystallizing the important corporation policies and making them effective, and to facilitate the adaptation of engineering improvements and operating methods, there are various so-called inter-divisional relations committees. They have suitable representation from the most important divisions, and are as follows: General Purchasing Committee, General Technical Committee, Works Managers Committee, General Sales Committee, Institutional Advertising Committee.

These committees meet separately at least once a month. The President of General Motors is a member of each one, and besides, there is at least one other member of the Executive Committee. The work of the committees clears through various central office staff organizations, maintained so as to perfect the flow of information back and forth and to facilitate the orderly consideration of common problems of important policy and procedure.

The Purchasing Committee deals with questions of general purchasing policy, but, by reason of the nature of the situation, it directs the actual purchasing arrangements in cases where it is found advantageous to centralize the purchases of materials common to two or more divisions. Such purchases usually are effected by a central staff organization headed by an executive who is secretary of the General Purchasing Committee. Similarly, the Institutional Advertising Committee passes upon copy for General Motors institutional advertising. In all other cases, however, the interdivisional relations committees have no actual authority. They are not designed to function as administrative bodies but rather as a means of providing an opportunity for general discussion of problems of common interest. No one is bound by the expression of opinion by others in meetings of these committees; there is no transfer of responsibility. Where there is a question at issue on the score of corporation policy the President of General Motors makes the decision or refers it to the Executive Committee for its determination. Cases of this kind are rare.

As a fundamental requisite in the work of coordination, it should be remembered that the bringing of men's minds together in connection with a given problem can always be greatly facilitated through a presentation of the facts. Disagreements fade away in proportion to the degree to which facts may be substituted for opinion. So far as it is practicable the discussions in these committees are predicated upon the display of facts. Questions of policy are clarified and through the operation of these several committees a means is provided of gaining a widely diffused knowledge and understanding of corporation policies, and a sympathetic compliance with them as they may bear upon the immediate problems of divisional management.

The head of each division should be qualified in every way to hold the position of president were its business owned and operated by an independent company. He has all the latitude and authority that normally would go with such a position, being limited only in the direction of policies such as properly would be dealt with by the board of directors or executive committee. In the actual situation such questions of policy are dealt with by the President of General Motors and group executives, facilitated through the operation of the various inter-divisional relations committees, reference being had to the Executive Committee of the Corporation when occasion requires.

        III   Public, Labor, Management and Capital, all Must Benefit

Business enterprise involves the welfare of four inter-dependent groups-the public, labor, management, and capital. Each must benefit from the efficiency of performance; to deprive any one group of that to which it is entitled would defeat its own object in the course of time. Control, with its object to secure the maximum economic efficiency in the employment of capital, is the essence of management. It means low economic cost of production and distribution. Control, to be effective, however, requires managerial ability such as commands, remuneration proportionate to its own economic contribution; its purpose is defeated unless the economic benefits are shared with the other three groups which are involved. Labor must be competent and well paid. The public, upon whom the business is dependent for economies resulting from volume, must be made aware of its beneficial enjoyment in the form of greater value for the purchasing dollar. With three of the groups, the public, labor, and management, enjoying their equitable share of the economic benefits of efficient management, capital can enjoy a measurably high rate of return as its reward.

The time available for this paper does not permit a description of all the various methods employed by General Motors in gaining effective control. However, the attempt is made to outline the general principles involved, and this would not be complete without touching upon the use of certain broad principles bearing upon compensation and treatment of executives and employees. Success requires men of the highest caliber and business ability, with breadth of viewpoint and understand of the interests of the stockholders. There must be the means to attract and to hold in the employ of the Corporation men of proven and potential ability, to the end that there may be progression from within in the perpetuation of sound management of the corporation and its various operating activities.

In 1923 the stockholders of General Motors Corporation approved a plan for the formation of the Managers Securities Company, designed to interest the men occupying important managerial positions as partners with the stockholders in the Corporation. Thereafter, the Managers Securities Company was incorporated, with a capital of $28,800,000 of 7% cumulative, non-voting preferred stock, and $5,000,000 of common stock. The common stock was sold to the men occupying important managerial positions in the General Motors Corporation for $5,000,000 cash. The Manager Securities Company then purchased the equivalent of 843,750 shares of present General Motors

Corporation common stock, paying therefor $40 per share (the then equivalent market price), aggregating a total purchase price of $33,750,000. In payment therefore the Managers Securities Company issued $28,800,000 of its 7% cumulative, non-voting preferred stock and paid the balance of $4,950,000 in cash.

The General Motors Corporation has a contract with the Managers Securities Company under which it agrees to pay to that company annually for each year from 1923 to 1930, both inclusive, 5% of its excess net earnings over and above 7% on the net capital employed. During the years 1923 to 1926 inclusive the net earnings of the Corporation available for dividends, including equities in subsidiary companies, aggregated $425,879,904, and there has been paid or accrued to the credit of Managers Securities Company under this agreement $15,923,943, which is equal to 3.74% of the net earnings of the Corporation.

This $15,923,943 is all that the General Motors Corporation has contributed, but in addition, at no cost whatever to the Corporation, there has been a substantial enhancement in the value of the common stock of the common stock of the General Motors Corporation purchased by the Managers Securities Company. This enhancement in the value of General Motors common shares has contributed greatly to the success of the Managers Securities Company plan and at the same time has resulted in great benefit to each and every common stockholder of General Motors Corporation.

To gain a sense of proportions it might be well to explain what "5% of excess net earnings over and above 7% on capital employed" means. The net capital employed by General Motors Corporation as of December 31, 1926, amounts to $637,454,214. The Corporation must earn 7% on this amount, of $44,621,795, before the Managers Securities Company receives anything. The Managers Securities Company for 1927 receives 5% of net earnings in excess of this $44,621,795. If the Corporation earned not more than $44,621,795, the Managers Securities Company would receive nothing, although the Corporation's net earnings would be equivalent to 5.83 times its preferred and debenture stock dividend requirements, leaving $36,973,503, which is equal to $4.25 on 8,700,000 shares of common stock outstanding.

There are about eighty executives owning stock of Managers Securities Company. The Directors of General Motors Corporation have expressed their belief that there has been no one influence contributing as much to the success of General Motors during the past four years as the keen interest evidenced in the Corporation's affairs by these eighty men occupying the most important managerial positions.

For ten or twelve years the Du Pont Company has been a larger holder of the common stock of General Motors Corporation. The 843,750 shares of General Motors common stock acquired by the Managers Securities Company in 1923 was purchased from the Du Pont Company. The enhancement in its market value in the meantime has been something like ninety-three million dollars. The Chairman of the Board of Du Pont Company recently referred jokingly to a remark of some one to the effect that that Company would be ninety odd million dollars better off if it had not sold that stock in 1923. His reply was that his company had enjoyed an enhancement in value of considerably over two hundred million dollars as applied to the General Motors stock which it holds as a permanent investment, and he saw no cause for complaint. The Du Ponts were far-seeing enough to make a part of their holdings in General Motors available for the constructive purposes of the Management Securities Company, having confidence in the belief that in the long run they would gain handsomely in consequence. They have learned from long experience in their own business to recognize the constructive benefits of ownership management. The incentive thus supplied is a vital force operating in the interest of all stockholders, since the stockholders at large inevitably enjoy a proportionate benefit of whatever is beneficial to the managing group.

Junior executives, heads of departments, and other employees occupying important positions, and from whom must be developed the senior executives of the future, obtain a partnership interest in the financial success of the institution as a whole through the operation of the Bonus Plan. The Bonus Plan, adopted in 1919, provides for annual awards of General Motors common stock as recognition of conspicuous and meritorious service.

Under the Bonus Plan, there is set aside each year five per cent of the amount by which the Corporation's earnings exceed 7% on the capital employed. Prior to the organization of Managers Securities Company, ten per cent of the earnings in excess of 7% on capital employed was set aside for bonus purposes, and the Bonus Plan embraced the Senior Executives, who are now participants in Managers Securities Company. The Bonus Fund is invested in General Motors common stock, and at the end of each year is allotted to the various operations on the basis of the extent to which each has contributed to the prosperity of the Corporation as a whole. Each operation in turn distributes its bonus allotment to eligible employees on the basis of the degree to which they have contributed to its success.

One-fourth of the stock so awarded is delivered at the time of the award, and the balance in three equal annual installments, provided the employee remains in the service of the Corporation.

All of the employees of the Corporation who have been in its service for three months are eligible to participate in the Savings and Investment Plan, which was established in 1919, the year following the adoption of the Bonus Plan. Under the Savings and Investment Plan, an employee may place into the Savings Fund each year an amount not exceed 20% of his annual wages or a maximum of $300. For each dollar paid by the employee into the Savings Fund, the Corporation pays fifty cents into the Investment Fund and the money paid by the Corporation into the Investment Fund is invested in common stock of the Corporation. Interest is credited to the employee semi-annually at the rate of 6% on the money he puts into the Savings Fund. A new class is started each year, and each class matures in five years. Means are provided whereby the employee may withdraw his entire savings plus accrued interest at any time he wishes, but in order to derive the full benefits from the Investment Fund contributed by the Corporation, he must remain in the service of the Corporation until the maturity of the class. The three classes started in 1919, 1920, and 1921 have now matured, and many employees, who originally paid $300 into each of these classes, or a total of $900, now have an accumulation of cash and securities having a total value of $9,838. Thus through the operation of this Saving and Investment Fund Plan a large number of employees have also become partners in the business, sharing as stockholders in the earnings of the Corporation and in the increased value of their holdings.

Each year the Corporation offers to all of its employees an opportunity for investing in not to exceed ten shares of 7% preferred stock, the number of shares allotted to each employee being dependent upon his salary. The subscription price is fixed each year, and payment may be made either in cash or in eleven equal monthly installments. Each of the shares held by employees carries an extra payment of $2.00 a share in addition to the regular $7.00 a share dividend. This plan is designed to afford an opportunity for the employees to make a safe investment, and to interest them further in the Corporation's financial success.

To further encourage employees to protect their dependents, there has been purchased a Group Life Insurance Policy under which employees who have been with General Motors at least three months may each obtain $1,000 life insurance, without medical examination. This insurance is payable at death to a designated beneficiary or in the event of permanent disability before the age of 60, to the employee, in 20 equal monthly installments. This Group Insurance Plan is cooperative, the employees and General Motors sharing the cost, and now covers approximately 96% of the eligible employees.

IV.   In Conclusion

In attempting to determine upon any important practice or procedure, it is important first to settle upon the fundamental principles which are involved. This paper is intended to deal with the fundamental principles involved in the problem of organization in corporation management. Most of the principles stated are generally acceptable; some possibly are controversial. At all events, it is essential to determine upon the fundamentals before proceeding towards a solution of the problem of centralized control with decentralized responsibilities. It is hoped that this paper will be of some help as a basis upon which a more detailed study of the problem may be carried on as applied to the particular conditions which surround a given industrial enterprise.